Precision & Pan

fine workmanship ~ fabulous details ~ outstanding quilts

Susan K Cleveland

Library of Congress Control Number 2011912888

ISBN 978-0-9792801-2-2

Published by Pieces Be With You®

54336 237th Ave

West Concord MN 55985 USA

www.PiecesBeWithYou.com

Printed by Palmer Printing in the USA

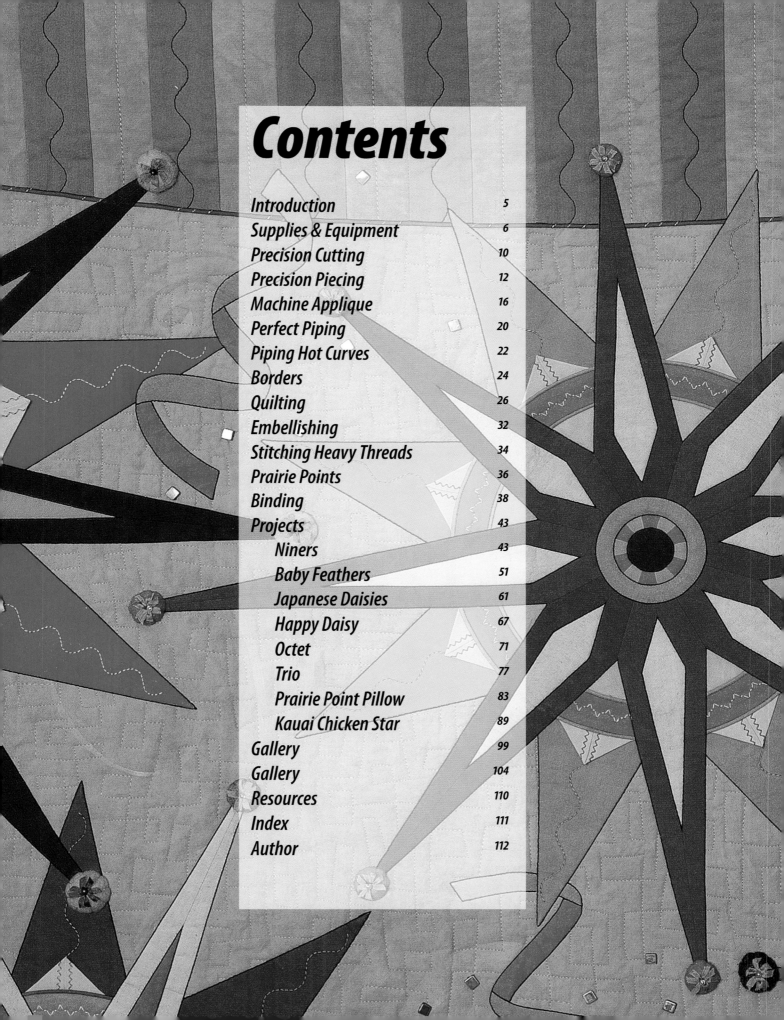

Contents

Acknowledgements

Photographer extraordinaire ~ Don Anderson of Anderson's Artistic Photography; Rochester, MN

Editor ~ Deborah K. Dayman

Test team and Contributors ~ Julie Antolak, Leitha Bothun, Heather Holtan, Synneva Hicks, Beth Holec, Kim Klocke, Barb Lovett, Lynne Majka, Judy Plank, Maureen Ruskell, Sharon Sandberg, Norma Sherwood, and Enid Gjelten Weichselbaum

Thanks

I try to remember to thank God every day for my wonderful life and gifts which I feel a responsibility to share.

A big thank you to my parents, Bob & Judy Lehms, who think I can accomplish anything...or at least lead me to believe that's what they think.

Thanks to my daughter, Erica, whose graphic design sense is fantastic.

Thanks to my son, Darin, who is both encouraging and understanding.

My dear quilting friends encourage my business endeavors and make a fuss over my quilts. All the success in the world would not be gratifying without buddies to share it with. Debbie, Norma, Sharon, Leitha, Judy, Beth, Kim, Barb, Nancy, Lynne, Emily, Julie, Enid, Maureen, Synneva, and Heather, I thank you. Sorry for my occasional whining.

Thank you to all my generous students and colleagues who make this business such a fun adventure.

Dedication

To my wonderful techno-hubby, Lee, who is still understanding of this compulsion of mine. We have a great life together.

Introduction

I've enjoyed teaching enthusiastic quilters for many years and it seems certain comments and questions repeatedly arise. Addressing these comments and answering these questions are my goals with this publication.

My work is noted for workmanship and attention to detail and to be honest, neither is a chore to me. Matching intersections, pointy points, straight border seams, and fussy details make me happy! Surely you understand, or you wouldn't be holding this book … the title would have scared you off.

Finding my quilting style was a blessing. When I learned how excruciating (only a slight exaggeration) free-motion quilting was for me, I decided to accentuate the positive and never mind the negative. I developed skills I enjoyed doing, and in doing so, found my niche.

Small quilts are my preference as I can use many techniques and see the light at the end of the tunnel. Several small projects are included in this book so you can practice the techniques shared.

My hope is that the techniques and patterns found within these pages will enhance *your* style and make you even more delighted with your quilting experiences and future masterpieces.

Q: I can't see where stitching starts and stops! How do you begin and end machine quilting lines?
A: page 28

Q: Those quilted circles are so round! How?
A: page 28

Q: Is there something inside that piping?
A: page 20

Q: I don't see the ditch quilting! How's that?
A: page 26

Q: I love the accent of piping in a border seam. Is that difficult?
A: page 24

Q: Are there tricks to piecing accurately?
A: page 12

Q: Who knew prairie points could be dramatic? Are they difficult to make?
A: page 36

Q: Those skinny pieced borders are so smooth. What makes them so?
A: page 24

Q: Oh, my dear! What is that fabulous thread?
A: page 34

Q: Good heavens—why don't you get a life?
A: Huh?

Supplies & Equipment

See *"Resources"* on page 110 for more information.

Fabric

Projects in this book contain 100% cotton fabric, polyester organza, and linen gauze. Quilts in the gallery include fabrics of wool and ultra-suede as well. There is no reason, however, that other fabrics can't get in on the fun. Test candidates to be sure they behave well when pressed/steamed, cut and sewn, then go for it.

Thread/ Needles

• **Piecing thread** ~ I recommend piecing with a good quality cotton thread of 50 weight (wt) or 60wt such as Superior Threads MasterPiece™ and 70/10 Jeans or Microtex needles.

• **Bobbin thread** ~ I always use 50wt or 60wt cotton in the bobbin. Winding a bobbin is fine, but I also like Superior Threads pre-wound bobbins of Master-Piece™ except when stitching with heavy decorative thread, then I wind a bobbin on my machine.

• **Thin threads** ~ For an invisible machine applique stitch, I choose lightweight threads such as WonderFil® InvisaFil™ (poly), YLI #100 silk, Superior

Threads Kimono Silk™ #100, or Superior Threads Bottom Line™ (poly). I use a 60/8 Microtex sewing machine needle.

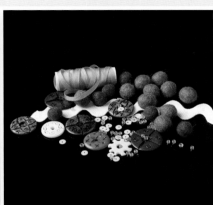

• **Heavy decorative threads** ~ An abundant supply of heavy decorative threads is available to us, but can be difficult to find. I've learned 30wt to 12wt threads stitch beautifully through the needle of a sewing machine and make bold hand quilting lines. They include: WonderFil Spagetti™ or Fruitti™ 12wt cotton, Superior Threads Tire brand #30 silk, YLI 1000 denier silk, Superior Threads #16 Quilter's silk, and Artfabrik 12wt pearl cotton. More fantastic threads are entering the marketplace as I write. Ooo-la-la!

Most machines prefer the 100/16 topstitch needle with heavy threads, but I usually try a 90/14 topstitch first as I like to get by with poking a smaller hole when possible. See *"Machine Stitching"* on page 34 .

For hand quilting, try between (quilting) needles size 7 or 8. Please see *"Hand Quilting"* on page 35.

• **Beading thread** ~ Silamide, FireLine® (both by Beadsmith®), and Nymo® are threads specifically designed for beads. They are available online or at beading shops.

• **Spiral Eye™ Side Threading Needles** ~ These are great for burying thread tails. They don't damage delicate threads or allow threads to pop out of the eye like some self-threading needles can. They are self-threading, but from the side rather than from the end.

Embellishments

• Oh, baby, the sky's the limit. I like beads of all sorts, felted wool balls, silk ribbon, sequins, … Test each treasure for heat tolerance and color fastness. See *"Embellishing"* on page 32.

Sewing Machines

• Good **speed control** is of utmost importance.

• **Needle positions** allow you to stitch a straight line with the needle right or left of center.

• **Needle down** is another valuable sewing machine feature. When "needle down" is set to "on", the needle will stop in the down position when you stop sewing. Your work will be held in place while you adjust your hands or reposition fabric.

• **Programmable presser foot lifter** is also an attractive feature. On some machines it is possible to program the *presser foot* when the "needle down" feature is engaged. You may want it to stop in the lifted position (to make pivoting easy) or in the down position (as usual, to hold fabric secure). What a treat!

• **Hands-free presser foot lifter** also allows the presser foot to be raised without removing your hands from your work. Most are operated by the right knee, though some are foot-controlled.

• An **open-toe foot** is a great aid. For many techniques it is necessary to see the needle and see clearly just in front of it. Making tiny piping with a **foot with a small groove** is a most enjoyable experience. A zipper foot can do the job, but not as well. A **built-in walking (or even-feed) foot** is one of my favorite features. It helps with precision piecing and it doesn't hop around in my face during quilting with my feed dogs up.

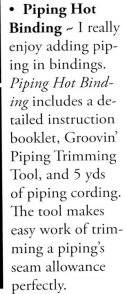

Other Supplies/ Equipment

• **Piping Hot Binding** ~ I really enjoy adding piping in bindings. *Piping Hot Binding* includes a detailed instruction booklet, Groovin' Piping Trimming Tool, and 5 yds of piping cording. The tool makes easy work of trimming a piping's seam allowance perfectly.

• **Piping Cording** ~ I use a poly 1/16″ cording in piped bindings and even smaller poly cording in the circles of Kauai Chicken Star (pictured on cover). Poly cording slides into the piping fabric nicely and has just the right amount of body … it's not too stiff nor too wobbly.

• **Prairie Pointer** ~ What else adds a bit of sassiness to a quilt like prairie points? This tool will help you make perfect prairie points every time and you'll enjoy every minute.

- **Rotary cutting equipment** ~ Look for rulers with thin lines which are broken frequently so you're able to see the fabric's edge clearly under a line. A solid line masks the fabric's edge. I want the line centered on the fabric's edge to create a perfect strip. Using the same brand of rulers throughout a project will maintain consistency.

Avoid shiny cutting mats and hard surface mats. Any of the others are great.

All cutters work well so the decision is personal preference. Changing your blade after each project will keep you from expending more energy than necessary while cutting.

- **Starch** ~ I find it beneficial to work with fabric having some body as distortion is much less of a problem. I like to use spray starch on fabrics after they've been washed and dried. Two or three light applications seem to work best.

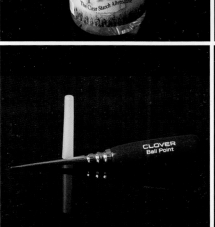

- **Starch alternative** ~ Mary Ellen's Best Press™ is a starch alternative that I love. Look for it in your favorite quilt shop. It doesn't flake or dirty an iron as spray starch can.

- **Iron** ~ If your pieces aren't pressing to a crisp fold, you may need a hotter iron. There are occasions when steam is helpful, but please remember to avoid steaming freezer paper as it will create a bond that must be completely saturated with water to loosen. This destroys freezer paper templates and wastes valu-

able time. Let's not discuss how this was discovered. It's OK. I'm over it.

- **Pressing surface** ~ A big pressing surface is quite valuable. Consider buying or making a large rectangular pressing surface to rest on top of your ironing board. I use a 4' x 3' pressing surface resting on a drawer unit. Steady Betty™ is a pressing surface that grabs fabric so it doesn't scoot away. It helps keep seams straight during pressing.

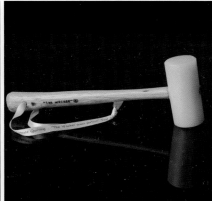

- **The Wacker** ~ This specially designed fabric smasher whacks bulky seam allowances down to slim and trim. Unfortunately, it doesn't work on thighs. I **love** this tool and feel every piecer should have one!

- **Pins** ~ Bohin extra-fine 0.40mm pins (part #26620) are amazing. They're so fine they allow for a very tiny bite of fabric. After bending, they straighten. Wow! Pins labeled "Quilter's Pins" are better suited to building a barn. Please don't make your fabric suffer with those.

- **Finger Cots** ~ Our hand/arm health is important. Using a finger cot on the finger used to pull the needle will reduce the pinch strength required and save our hands! I use one on my non-sewing thumb also to hold binding in place as I sew. Finger cots may be found at your quilt shop or in the drug store near the suppositories. I'd go for the quilt shop. For a much longer lasting alternative, I strongly recommend Bohin Finger Cots for Quilting #91720–91722. They are thin enough to feel the needle in your grip whereas a similar product, librarian's page-turners, are not.

- **Stiletto (awl)** ~ When accuracy is the goal, a stiletto can help guide pieces through the machine as they approach the needle. The Clover Ball Point Awl is my favorite as it is pointy enough to guide fabric but doesn't poke holes in fabric — or in me.

- **Fabric scissors** ~ Karen Kay Buckley's Perfect Scissors™ are, well, perfect. One blade is serrated so fabric is pulled in rather than pushed out and they cut all the way to the tippy tip.

- **Wonder Clips®** ~ Clover® has come up with a better clip to hold binding in place as it is sewn to the back of the quilt. How wonderful! (part #3155–3156)

- **Post-it Notes®** ~ Use as a guide on the bed of the sewing machine when piecing or making piping. How the pioneers pieced quilts without Post-it Notes® and freezer paper is beyond me.

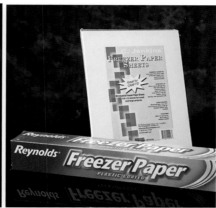

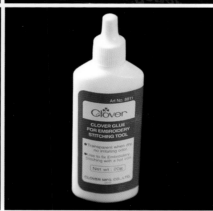

- **Freezer paper** ~ As I understand it, long, long ago freezer paper was used for storing uncooked meat. Thankfully, we've realized the real reason for freezer paper's existence…for quilting. Freezer paper is one of the most valuable tools in my quilting room. I use it for a multitude of quilting tasks: marking quilting designs, piecing, and applique.

Freezer paper shrinks! To pre-shrink, iron it shiny side down to a pressing surface until it sticks. Peel it up and then use it.

Some quilt shops now carry freezer paper in sheets sized to be used in an ink jet printer. I prefer C Jenkins brand as it's a heavier paper. Rolls may be purchased in quilt shops or the food storage section of grocery stores.

A seriously hot dry iron is necessary for adhering freezer paper to fabric. Old freezer paper will not adhere to fabric well. If freezer paper isn't staying on your fabric, your iron is not hot enough or the freezer paper should be in a museum.

- **Fusible web** ~ There are many fusible webs on the market. Ask someone at your quilt shop for a recommendation or go with **Pellon® Decor-Bond®**. My friend, Mickey Depre of www.mdquilts.com, turned me on to this. Decor-Bond is a fairly heavy interfacing, so background prints will not shadow through and appliques seem to hover over the quilt's surface. It has adhesive only on one side and it's a bit firm, but not too firm. It stays in place nicely as one side is fused to the applique and the other side clings to the background as it's stitched. Give it a try!

- **Fabric glue** ~ Clover Glue for Embroidery Stitching Tool is useful to hold prairie points in place before they're sewn and to secure thread ends. It is permanent, dries clear, and is thick enough to not soak through to front of fabric. (part #8811)

Precision Cutting

Cutting Crosswise-grain Strips

Most strips will be cut cross-grain. If instructions don't mention grainline, it is assumed strips will be cut on the crosswise grain.

Fabric should be pre-washed, dried and starched prior to cutting. See *"Starch"* and *"Starch Alternative"* on page 8. Sometimes I don't pre-wash medium- or light-value fabrics but simply press with steam and then starch and press again. This will pre-shrink fabric but won't provide protection from colors running.

• Fold fabric as it came off the bolt, selvage to selvage. Hold selvages in the air out in front of yourself and slide selvages back and forth until the fabric hangs straight.

• Lay folded piece on cutting mat with fold either near yourself or away.

• Place line of ruler on fold and make cut to straighten rough end. Cross-grain strips will be cut from this edge.

• Leave ruler on fabric and fold extra yardage up onto mat.

• Spin mat, extra yardage and ruler.

• Unfold extra yardage and cut strips as needed being careful not to disturb cut edge.

• **Cut strips aligning fabric's edge under appropriate line of ruler. Use broken (dashed) line of ruler to center fabric's edge under the line and create perfect strips. The *turn of the cloth* will be accounted for in the seam allowance rather than during cutting.** Please see *"Precision Piecing"* on page 12.

• After about 4–5 strips have been cut, turn mat again and check to be sure cut edge is perpendicular to fold. Cut a fresh edge if needed, then turn mat, and continue cutting strips.

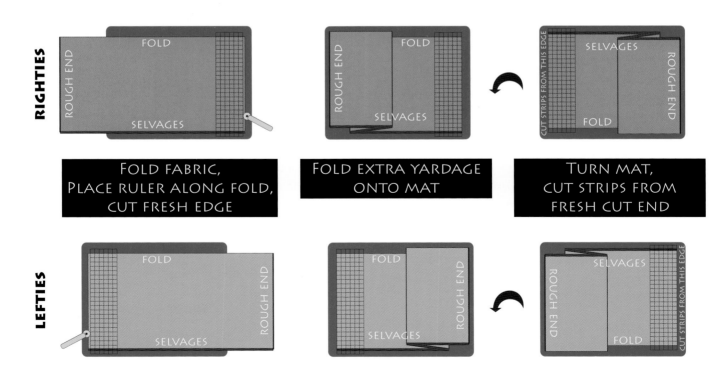

RIGHTIES

FOLD FABRIC, PLACE RULER ALONG FOLD, CUT FRESH EDGE

FOLD EXTRA YARDAGE ONTO MAT

TURN MAT, CUT STRIPS FROM FRESH CUT END

LEFTIES

Cutting Lengthwise-grain Strips

• Straighten first end as described earlier. Turn mat and fabric, slide other end of fabric onto mat and straighten other end.

• Unfold fabric and re-fold cut edge to cut edge.

• Straighten edge with folded selvages in same way first end was straightened. If the piece is too wide for the ruler, bring cut edges to fold before aligning ruler to make cut. Strips will be cut from this edge.

• Leave ruler on piece and fold extra yardage up onto mat.

• Spin mat and extra yardage.

• Unfold extra yardage and cut strips as needed from this fresh cut.

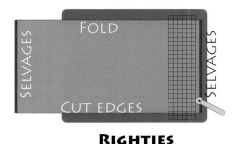

RIGHTIES

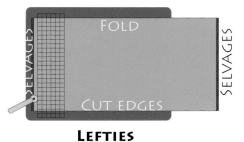

LEFTIES

STRAIGHTEN END FOR CUTTING LENGTHWISE-GRAIN STRIPS THEN SPIN MAT AND CUT STRIPS FROM THIS FRESH CUT

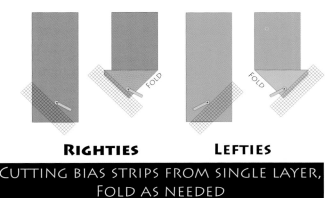

RIGHTIES   **LEFTIES**

CUTTING BIAS STRIPS FROM SINGLE LAYER, FOLD AS NEEDED

Cutting Bias Strips

• Lay single layer of fabric on cutting mat.

• Place 45 degree line of ruler along selvage.

• Make first cut, then cut strips from this edge. When ruler no longer reaches from edge to edge, fold fabric as shown (cut edge over itself) to make more cuts.

Tip: Rotary cutter test: At the beginning of each project, expose the cutter's blade and roll it along your cutting mat. If the cutter does not turn easily, place one finger on the hub and loosen the nut (remember lefty-loosey, righty-tighty). Cutting with a tight cutter will require more energy than using a free-wheeling cutter.

Precision Piecing

There's more fun to be had when pieces fit together nicely and more time is spent sewing rather than ripping. These tips can make a world of difference.

• If fabrics have not been pre-washed, steam press and use starch or Best Press before cutting. Fabrics with body will distort less and the steam will pre-shrink fabrics.

• Please see *"Piecing Thread"* on page 6 for information on thread and needles.

• A stiletto or the Clover Ball Point Awl is quite valuable to guide fabrics through the machine and keep fingers safe.

• When joining pieces together, take time to assure edges are lined up perfectly. If the bottom piece is light in value and your

sewing table is light, it's difficult to verify alignment. Either flip the pieces so a darker piece is on the bottom, or place something darker under your pieces so alignment is easier to see. I placed a bright-colored Post-it Note under the clear surround of my machine making it easier to see that fabric edges are aligned perfectly.

• Check the height of your sewing machine's surround. A difference in height could cause seam allowances to get caught and flip during sewing.

Adjust the height of the machine or surround so the surfaces are even. If this is not possible, make a ramp with a couple of Post-it Notes with the sticky edge farthest from the machine. If your machine has a drop-in bobbin, there may be a divot in front of the needle that could be a problem. The Post-it Note ramp will help with this also.

• Taping your sewing machine's surround to the machine will keep it in place. The surround tends to wiggle away from the machine during sewing and if a seam guide is used, it travels too and becomes inaccurate.

• Stitch length needs to be small enough to hold pieces tightly and not cause problems if one or two stitches let go at the beginning or end of a seam. I like piecing with a 2.0mm stitch length (12-15 stitches per inch).

• Usually the machine's general, or all-purpose foot is the best choice for piecing because it holds fabric flat when a stitch is formed. However, when working with triangles and mitered borders/sashings, an open-toe foot is better so the stitching path can be seen clearly.

Some ¼"-feet don't align with a machine's feed dogs well in order to properly feed fabric through the machine. It might behoove you to check yours.

• When piecing long strips and machine quilting straight lines, I set the machine to stop with the **needle down and foot down**. It's helpful when stopping to adjust fabric in the middle of a seam because the needle and foot help hold fabric in place. Some machines won't stop with both down, but most will. It may require some investigative work and your machine's manual to learn about this.

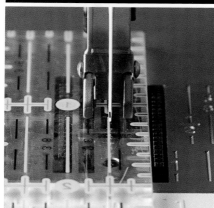

• When chain piecing I set the machine to stop with the **needle down and foot up**. When the needle is down, feed dogs are down and out of the way. This allows new pieces to be placed under the foot up to the needle before sewing. Otherwise, the foot will knock carefully aligned pieces out of alignment because it hits the leading edge of the top piece.

• Pay particular attention to the beginning and ending of each seam. Don't allow stitches to wander in these areas. ¼" from the end of every seam is most important because that's where subsequent seams will cross.

• *Take advantage of the right feed dog!* You may be surprised to learn that when piecing with the needle in the center position, fabric is probably not totally covering the right feed dog. (This is true of nearly all machines.) I liken this situation to driving with your car's right wheels in the mud. Move your needle to the right (and your seam guide also) so that all feed dogs are moving fabric straight through the machine. You'll be surprised what a difference this makes! … more later.

NEEDLE MOVED TO RIGHT TO USE FEED DOGS WHEN STITCHING ¼" SEAM

Scant ¼" Seam Allowance

When seam allowances are pressed to one side, one fabric folds back on itself and up over the thread. The amount of fabric taken up in the fold is the **turn of the cloth**.

If strips are cut perfectly, then a perfect ¼" seam allowance would yield a **result too small** because some fabric is taken up in the turn of the cloth. So, the seam allowance must be a scant ¼", but how scant?

Fabric thickness and thread thickness are each part of the equation. In theory thicker threads and thicker fabrics take up more fabric in the turn of the cloth and require a smaller seam allowance in order for the resulting measurement to be correct. If you've struggled with a ¼"-foot, perhaps this explains the problem. Perhaps it was not calibrated for the specific fabrics and thread you're working with.

Whether seams are pressed open or to one side affects the final measurement as well. Seams pressed open use slightly less in the turn of the cloth and may require a different seam allowance.

We don't care what the seam allowance measures. We care that pieces sewn together yield the correct measurement!

I cut strips as perfectly as possible and account for turn of the cloth in the seam allowance. For instance, when cutting a 2" strip, I center the 2" line of the ruler over the fabric's cut edge. I don't lay the 2" line up onto the fabric which creates a strip that's a bit wider than 2".

TURN OF
THE CLOTH

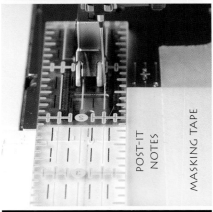

POST-IT NOTES

MASKING TAPE

PLACE POST-IT NOTES
FOR SEAM GUIDE

Machine Set-up

Machine set-up must be done with fabrics from the actual project, stitching with thread from the actual project, and measuring with the ruler from the actual project.

To set up your machine for an accurate seam allowance:

• Remove the foot.

• Move the machine's needle nearly all the way to the right in order to **take advantage of the right feed dog** and enable the machine to feed fabric straight through the machine.

• Turn an acrylic ruler upside down so the paint is up. Place it under the needle and **lower the needle down to touch the right edge of the ¼" line** (scant ¼"). Check lines on machine bed to be sure ruler is straight and be careful not to bend the needle. When ruler is straight, lower foot shank to help hold ruler in place if possible. (For best results, use a ruler the same brand as others used in your project.)

• Place 4–5 Post-it Notes beside ruler with sticky edge beside ruler. Add tape to secure.

• Remove ruler and replace foot on machine.

• Cut a perfect 1½" strip from a fabric in your project and cut it into several approximate 3" or 4" segments.

• Align edges carefully and sew 2 pieces together. Press seam allowance to one side then add another piece. Press seam allowance to one side. Check to be sure there are no pouty lips (flaps) along seam line.

• Measure resulting width. It should measure 3½" exactly. Measure across the middle of the strip set and don't use the end of the ruler but measure from line to line.

• If result is too big, then the seam allowance needs to be a bit larger. Remove Post-it Notes and lower needle to ruler into **center** of ¼″ line. If result is too small, then the seam allowance needs to be a bit smaller. Remove Post-it Notes and lower needle to ruler just **right** of ¼″ line. Re-test.

• If a variety of fabrics is used in one project, test with the most frequently used weight of fabric.

Pressing

• Set iron at highest setting for fabric content.

• Use a pressing surface that's not too firm so pieces don't slide away from the iron and not too soft so pieces don't sink down and distort. The Steady Betty is a pressing surface that clings to fabrics and makes it easier to keep strips straight while pressing seam allowances to one side.

• Set seam flat first.

• Press seam allowance in direction of fewest seams and/or to ease construction so seam intersections have abutting seams.

• Use the side of the iron to knock fabric over being careful to keep strips/pieces straight.

• Be especially careful at beginning and end of seam lines so they don't distort. Use lighter pressure in those areas.

• Steam if necessary but use with extreme caution because steam makes fabric vulnerable to distortion.

• The Wacker is a fabulous tool to reduce bulk at intersections. Once you wack, you'll never go back (to not wacking).

• When piecing strip sets for skinny borders or small half-square triangles, I press seams open. A tiny, 1.5mm stitch length will keep stitches from showing. Pressing these seams open distributes bulk and flatter pieced areas result. Please see *Niners* on page 43, *Trio* on page 77, and *Baby Feathers* on page 51 for examples of pressing seams open.

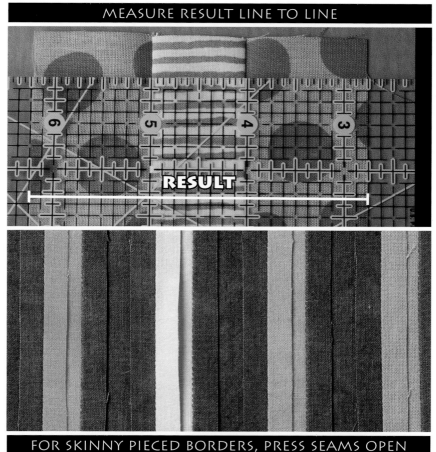

MEASURE RESULT LINE TO LINE

RESULT

FOR SKINNY PIECED BORDERS, PRESS SEAMS OPEN

BIG NEWS: The Quilter's Custom Seam Guide is in development as this book is going to print! Please visit www.PiecesBeWithYou.com for more information.

Circle Applique - invisible

Kauai Chicken Star on cover and quilts in the gallery include examples of invisible machine applique.

- Make a double-thick freezer paper template the size of the finished circle. These templates may not be re-used. For re-usable circle templates please use Perfect Circles by Karen Kay Buckley.

} To make a double-thick freezer paper template:

» Pre-shrink two pieces of freezer paper by ironing each to pressing surface, shiny side down with a dry iron, then peel off of surface.

» Iron one pre-shrunk piece to pressing surface, then iron a second pre-shrunk piece on top, let cool, then peel off surface.

» Use circle template to draw circle, then cut OR use a circle cutter.

» Punch a hole near center of template.

- Cut fabric ½" larger than finished circle (¼" seam allowance).

- Use doubled thread to stitch a running stitch (by hand) around fabric circle near its edge overlapping a few stitches at beginning/ending (make sure stitches match over/under).

- Place template on wrong side of fabric (no need to press in place).

- Pull running stitches tight until template slightly curls, knot thread, and even out gathers.

- Place fabric circle right side up onto right side of background and tape in place.

- Set up machine with 60/8 Microtex needle and thin thread using 0.5–0.8mm wide x 1.0–1.5mm long zig-zag.

Stitch, removing tape as necessary. Left swing of needle should just barely catch circle fabric. Stop to pivot frequently with needle in background. If possible, set machine to stop with needle down and foot up to make pivoting easy. Please see *"Thin Threads"* on page 6.

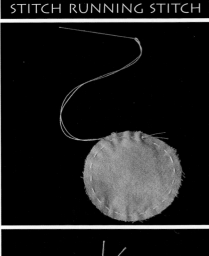

USE DOUBLED THREAD STITCH RUNNING STITCH

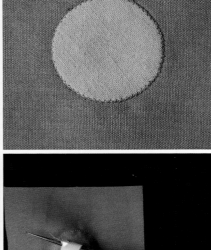

WITH THIN THREAD, ZIG-ZAG IN PLACE

TEMPLATE ON WRONG SIDE, PULL STITCHES, KNOT

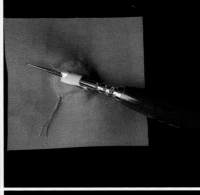

SLIT BACK, REMOVE TEMPLATE

- From wrong side, carefully cut slit in background fabric under circle. Insert Clover Ball Point Awl or other not-so-pointy tool into slit and through punched hole. Sweep under circle template and pop template out.

- To finish, pull threads to wrong side, tie off and/or dot with permanent glue such as Clover Glue for Embroidery Stitching Tool. See *"Fabric Glue"* on page 9.

- Press gently on padded surface.

- Outline with heavy decorative thread by machine now or during quilting through all layers (optional, but worth the time). Please see *"Heavy Decorative Threads"* on page 6 and *"Stitching with Heavy Threads"* on page 34.

Seam allowances left intact help give dimension to circles. Another way to get circles to pop is to hand quilt around them. Give hand quilting thread a little extra tug and circles will pop!

Other Fun Options

- Stack appliqueed circles! To stack, begin with the top circle and work down as in *Kauai Chicken Star* project on page 89.

- Piece circles to be appliqueed. I foundation piece onto freezer paper, then applique other circles over it as in *Psychedelic Big Bang* (lower right corner) and on page 99.

- Turn under edges of any shape and applique with thin thread and a zig-zag stitch, then during quilting, use a heavy decorative thread to outline shapes as in *Psychedelic Big Bang* (lower left corner) and on page 99.

- Embellish circle fabric before making circles as in *Twirling Tassels* (top right corner) and on page 103, and in *Bouncin'* on page 100. *Twirling Tassels'* circles are hand-stitched with silk ribbon and heavy silk thread while

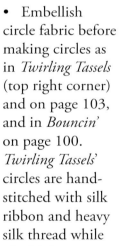

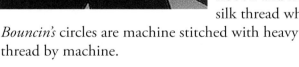

Bouncin's circles are machine stitched with heavy thread by machine.

Decorative Thread Applique

Japanese Daisies on page 61, *Happy Daisy* on page 67, and many quilts in the gallery include examples of decorative thread applique.

When an edge is to be covered with decorative thread, I choose raw-edged fusible applique.

Please see *"Heavy Decorative Threads"* on page 6 for information on threads available and *"Stitching Heavy Threads"* on page 34 for stitching tips.

• There are many good choices for securing applique pieces to background fabric. As with most products, I suggest testing it with your fabrics to be sure the product adheres well and adhesive dots do not show through the fabric. My super-smart quilting teacher friend, Mickey Depre, suggests using an unconventional product, Pellon Decor-Bond for fusible applique. Give it a try! Please see *"Pellon Decor-Bond"* on page 9.

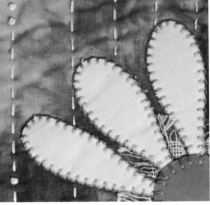

Trace reverse image of applique shapes to paper side of fusible web or dull side of Pellon Decor-Bond then press to wrong side fabric. Cut on line and place on project. Please follow manufacturer's instructions to avoid brutal disappointment.

• Heavy decorative threads are listed in *"Heavy Decorative Threads"* on page 6. 30wt and 12wt per-

form best for decorative applique as they are able to bend back on themselves better than heavier threads.

• A 100/16 topstitch needle will give great results, but I first try a 90/14 topstitch needle in order to see if I can poke a smaller hole. Sometimes it works.

• The most popular stitch patterns for decorative applique are the blanket stitch and the modest zig-zag. Experiment with stitch pattern, stitch length and width for different effects. It's great fun!

• Stitch placement can be a variable too. I like my stitch pattern to just barely go over the applique's edge, but centering the stitch pattern on the edge can also be attractive.

• Please be sure to starch background fabric with several applications of starch or use a light-weight fusible interfacing so fabric has some firmness. It needs to survive pokings by a large needle. Tear-away stabilizers are not a good option as threads could break during tear-away. These stitches must be large to be appropriate for the thread's size.

• Test on a scrap before stitching on your project! These big needles leave holes, so removing stitches is not a good idea. After cutting out applique pieces, I save the leftovers. They are negative images of the applique and already have fusible on them. Press onto on a scrap of background and stitch. Adjust stitch pattern, width, length, and tension to your liking. I suggest increasing width and length from the machine's default settings in order to show off the beautiful thread.

• To begin and end stitching, simply pull thread tails to back of work. Tie off and/or dot with permanent glue. I prefer Clover Glue for Embroidery Stitching Tool. It's permanent after heat set, dries clear and doesn't soak through to the front of fabric. (I don't know what an Embroidery Stitching Tool is, but I like this glue.) Please see *"Fabric Glue"* on page 9.

• Most importantly, stop to pivot as often as needed with the needle down in the background fabric. Sometimes I stop and pivot after each stitch if the curve is tight. This creates a smooth, beautiful curve.

Extras:

• For a thrill, try stuffing appliques with wool! Press and steam a scrap of 100% wool batting until it's flat — really flat. Cut a piece just a bit smaller than the applique. Place on background then place applique piece over it and stitch. As the piece is handled, the wool will poof a bit. This was done on the daisy projects found on pages 61 and 67.

• Thread color impacts the look of applique greatly. Subtly contrasting thread adds texture, but the boldness of high contrast and a thick outline may be just the design element the applique piece needs.

• After appliqueing, quilt around pieces with a thin thread or add an extra pop with a contrasting heavy decorative thread as in *Hippie Daisies* on page 107.

Perfect Piping

Nearly every quilt in this book includes an example of perfect piping (if I do say so myself).

I use piping in three different ways and each requires a different technique. All are fussy but worth the effort!

To learn how to insert piping into a border seam, please see *"Borders"* on page 24 and *Kauai Chicken Star* project on page 89.

To learn how to insert piping into curves, please see

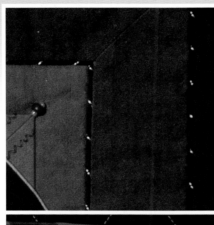

"Piping Hot Curves" on page 22 and *Kauai Chicken Star* project on page 89.

To learn how to create perfectly piped bindings, please refer to *Piping Hot Binding,* a kit containing a detailed booklet, Groovin' Piping Trimming Tool, and cording. See *"Resources"* on page 110.

{ *Tip: Embellished piping is one of my favorite tricks. Stitch lines on piping fabric (straight of grain) before it is cut into bias strips. Note that stitching lines will appear farther apart after bias is cut. I think it makes Kauai Chicken Star really sparkle! Please don't worry for me—I'm aware I'm not well.* }

Prepare Piping Fabric / Cording

• Cut appropriate number of 1¼" bias strips. Please see *"Cutting Bias Strips"* on page 11.

• Splice strips. Place right sides together making the corner of a square and sew from crevasse to crevasse. Allow extra length to extend beyond intersection. The angles of the strips' ends don't matter. Use 1.5mm stitches, press seam allowances open and trim to about ¼".

• Press strip in half the long way, wrong sides together. Leaving cut edges slightly askew will make it easier to open the strip and insert cording.

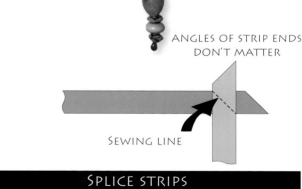

ANGLES OF STRIP ENDS
DON'T MATTER

SEWING LINE

SPLICE STRIPS

**PRESS WRONG
SIDES TOGETHER**

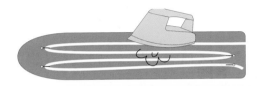

STEAM CORDING TO PRE-SHRINK

• Pre-shrink cording with steam. I put a pin in one end of cording and wind it around pins back and forth on my pressing surface, then hover over it with the iron and steam. (Pins simply keep the cording from tangling as it shrinks.) I move pins as necessary as cording shrinks. If you don't see cording shrink, then your iron isn't hot enough to shrink the cording. When/if you steam your quilt later, it won't shrink then either. It's OK.

Sew Perfect Piping

• Thread machine with slightly contrasting thread.

• Place foot on machine. A foot with a small groove is preferred but a zipper foot will do.

• Tie a knot in end of cording and tuck cording tightly into piping fabric's fold.

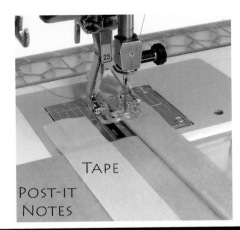

TAPE

POST-IT NOTES

LOWER FOOT ONTO PIPING
ADJUST NEEDLE POSITION
PLACE POST-IT NOTES® BESIDE FOLD

• Lower foot over piping. If using a zipper foot place foot beside cording. If using a foot with a groove, place groove over cording.

• Place 8–10 Post-it Notes® beside fold and just in front of feed dogs. Secure with tape. This will keep piping feeding into the machine straight —— no more lumpy piping.

• Adjust needle position to stitch near cording with 2.0mm stitch length. (Check your machine's manual if you're not familiar with needle positions.)

Tip: Leave enough space for another stitching line between this stitching and cording. If your fingernail just barely fits between cording and stitching, that's great. Take time setting up the machine for great results..

GROOVIN' PIPING TRIMMING TOOL

TRIM SEAM ALLOWANCE

• Pull cording into fold and work a few inches at a time. Smooth piping is more important than tight piping. Do not catch cording in stitching.

• Trim seam allowance to ¼". The Groovin' Piping Trimming Tool makes this task quick, easy, and precise. See *"Resources"* on page 110.

Piping Hot Curves

This technique is included in the *Kauai Chicken Star* project on page 89 and in many quilts in the gallery.

While this is a brief overview of the technique I developed, I invite you to reference *Piping Hot Curves* by Susan K Cleveland, published by Pieces Be With You, for detailed instructions and many projects showcasing piping in curves.

Feel free to make your own curvy templates and add piped curves in your projects!

• Make a triple-thick freezer paper template of desired curve.

》 Pre-shrink three pieces of freezer paper by ironing each to pressing surface, shiny side down with a dry iron, then peel off of surface.

》 Trace or draw curve on one pre-shrunk piece.

》 Iron one plain pre-shrunk piece to pressing surface, then iron a second plain pre-shrunk piece on top, then iron printed piece on top, let cool, then peel off surface. All should be shiny side down.

》 Cut on drawn line.

• Make piping using contrasting thread in needle and matching thread in bobbin then trim seam allowance to ¼". See *"Perfect Piping"* on page 20.

• Iron triple-thick freezer paper template to right side of fabric. Rough cut fabric ½" from curved edge (optional).

• Place trimmed piping **beside** template with fold of piping **beside** template, matching thread down and contrasting thread up so it can be seen. Stitch beside cording (closer than original stitching line) with an open-toe foot and 1.5mm stitches. Sometimes a groovy foot is able to perform this task, but usually the groove is straight and we're stitching curves. (If a continuous circle is needed, bend beginning tail into seam allowance and stitch piping to overlap beginning, then bend ending tail into seam allowance.)

• If shadowing is not an issue with this fabric, trim fabric's seam allowance a bit smaller than piping's seam allowance but if this fabric has a shadowing issue, trim its seam allowance a bit bigger than piping's seam allowance.

PRESS TEMPLATE TO RIGHT-SIDE FABRIC

RIGHT SIDE

TRIM SEAM, PRESS SEAMS TO WRONG SIDE

WRONG SIDE

APPLY TRIMMED PIPING BESIDE TEMPLATE

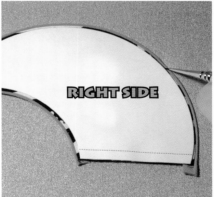

DIG DITCH THEN RE-PRESS

RIGHT SIDE

• From wrong side of piped piece, press seam allowances to wrong side, flip piece over, drag pointy object such as the Clover Ball Point Awl in ditch to smooth curve and push cording out into the piping's fold. Press again. This step is very important! Don't be alarmed to see that piping is about ⅛″ from the edge of the freezer paper template. That's correct. All is well.

• Place piped shape onto right side of background, tape in place and stitch in ditch with thin (or invisible) thread and a small 60/8 Microtex needle using 1.5mm stitches. Remove tape as needed. Please see *"Thin Threads"* on page 6.

Please see *"Thin Threads"* on page 6.

TIP: When stitching in the ditch, hold a pointy tool in the ditch just ahead of the machine's needle. Hold it steady and do not let it move. It will open the ditch slightly and allow the needle to get down into the ditch where stitches will be hidden.

• Remove template and cut background from behind piped shape if reducing bulk if desired. If shadowing is occurring, the background **must** be trimmed from behind piped shape.

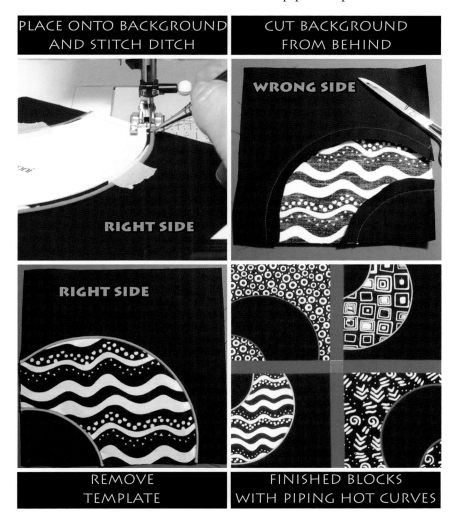

PLACE ONTO BACKGROUND AND STITCH DITCH

RIGHT SIDE

CUT BACKGROUND FROM BEHIND

WRONG SIDE

RIGHT SIDE

REMOVE TEMPLATE

FINISHED BLOCKS WITH PIPING HOT CURVES

Borders

Squared Borders

This technique is included in the *Niners* project on page 43, *Baby Feathers* project on page 51 and in many quilts in the gallery.

Borders must be carefully applied so that quilts lay flat. Borders cut on the lengthwise grain (parallel to selvage) are less vulnerable to stretching or distortion. Please see *"Cutting Lengthwise-grain Strips"* on page 11.

I prefer adding longest borders first (sides for a tall quilt, top/bottom for a wide quilt).

• Measure quilt's width or length (whichever is longest) through the center. Use the same tape measure or ruler which will be used to cut border to length. Edges may have stretched, so measuring through the center is a more accurate measurement.

• Cut border accurately to length.

• Pin to quilt matching ends and centers, then every 2–3".

TRIM TO PROPER WIDTH AFTER SEWING TO QUILT BODY

• Sew, then press seam allowance toward piece with fewest seams. If points need to meet border seam, sew with pieced unit on top and adjust sewing to intersect points. Note: When pressing border seams, be gentle at the ends. They tend to distort.

• Repeat for top/bottom or sides.

Skinny Pieced Borders

This technique is included in *Niners* on page 43, *Baby Feathers* on page 51, and *Trio* on page 77.

Oh, a skinny pieced border is a beautiful thing! Here's the big picture. Build border strip sets much wider than what is needed—one strip set for top/bottom borders and one strip set for right/left borders. Trim one long edge to create a clean edge, then sew to quilt and press. Trim a certain distance from the border seam and reuse remaining strip set. The *certain distance* is the intended finished border width plus one seam allowance.

Working with a wide strip set reduces chances for stretching. Once the pieced border is sewn to the quilt, it's more stable and may be trimmed. Smart, huh?

Skinny pieced border strip sets should be pieced with tiny, 1.5mm stitches so when seam allowances are pressed open, stitches won't show. Seams are pressed open to distribute bulk. No one wants unsightly bulges in a pieced border.

When measuring, measure through the center of the quilt and center of border strip set. Edges may have stretched.

The quilt or border strip set will be trimmed or adjusted to fit perfectly.

Borders with Piping

Special responsibilities accompany adding piping in a border seam. It's like getting a puppy. Extra time and attention is required to make everything go smoothly, and if you're not willing to make the commitment, don't go there lest you end up with wavy piped border seams or stained carpet. Got it?

Special responsibilities:

» First, you must be willing (and able) to quilt (through all layers) in the piping's ditch in order to keep this seam straight. This stitching must be down in the ditch between the piping and the new border. See *"In-the-ditch Quilting"* on page 26.

» Second, you must be willing to avoid dense quilting. When a quilt is quilted to the point of being bullet proof, it draws up. This is a problem. Corded piping will not draw up and it must go somewhere, so it mimics the Rocky Mountains amidst dense quilting. This is not attractive.

In border seams, I strongly recommend using tiny, 1/16″ cording so that intersections don't get bulky where pipings cross. Tiny piping is very impressive and a smart fabric choice will attract attention from across the room.

• Make piping and trim seam allowance to 1/4″. Please see *"Perfect Piping"* on page 20.

• Place piping at edge of block or quilt and stitch exactly over piping stitching line. Leave a little extra piping at the corners. It will be trimmed later. Cross over pipings in corners to create crisp corners. Trim excess piping at corners.

• Cut border to length, place over piping (right sides together) and pin in place. Flip entire piece over and sew one thread left of the stitching line that is securing piping in place. This seam will not be the perfect scant 1/4″ seam, so you may wish to cut the border wider than needed and trim it later to a perfect finished width. When it comes to borders, I measure and cut each to the proper length, so loosing the perfect scant 1/4″ seam is not an issue here.

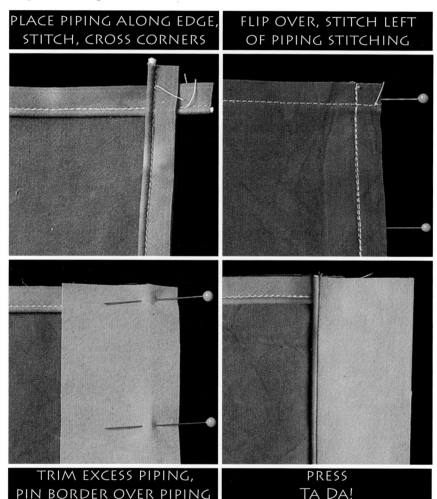

PLACE PIPING ALONG EDGE, STITCH, CROSS CORNERS

FLIP OVER, STITCH LEFT OF PIPING STITCHING

TRIM EXCESS PIPING, PIN BORDER OVER PIPING

PRESS TA DA!

Marvelous Miters.

• Press seam toward new border and please don't forget the special responsibilities associated with a piped border seam. (This was written with my finger pointed at you for added emphasis. Not really … I was typing, but doesn't that produce a scary visual.)

Mitered Borders

Mitered borders add an impressive touch to any quilt. I have developed a simple and reliable technique which I share in my book

Tip: Embellished piping is one of my favorite tricks! In Kauai Chicken Star (cover and page 89), I stitched "stripes" on a piece of solid hand-dyed black fabric with 30wt silk thread before cutting it up. If you've been accused of being anal retentive with your quilting, you may enjoy this also.

Quilting

I think of quilting as two distinct types: structural (in-the-ditch) quilting and decorative quilting. Each performs a specific task. One keeps straight seams straight and emphasizes edges of elements by "nailing" them down into the quilt sandwich. The other enhances the quilt top, fills empty spaces, and offers interest while the quilt is admired up close.

Preparing the Quilt Sandwich

The first step in successful quilting? Press all seam allowances well during construction …no pouty-lip seams. Use the Wacker seams perfect™ on intersections to reduce bulk (and to relieve frustrations). Press normally from the right side, steam, steam, WACK, WACK, steam once again. Let the piece cool before touching it. You'll be absolutely amazed at how flat your quilt top can be. It's much easier to ditch quilt a nice flat piece. (Some machines even skip stitches where bulk occurs. Yikes!)

When the quilt top is finished, I suggest placing it on a pressing surface wrong side up and giving it a final press to assure all seams are pressed in the direction intended. Remove any loose threads as they may show through the quilt top and are very difficult to remove after quilting. Use starch or Best Press to give the quilt top a little body.

Layer quilt top, batting and backing, then baste with safety pins in about a 4″ grid. At the sew-

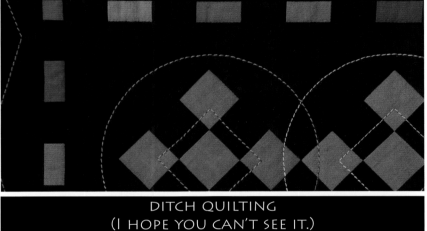

DITCH QUILTING
(I HOPE YOU CAN'T SEE IT.)

ing, machine stay-stitch the quilt's edge. Engage the built-in walking foot or install the walking foot. Machine sew each edge through all layers less than ¼″ from the edge of the quilt top. Use a big stitch length (3.0mm) and contrasting thread. Don't turn corners, but rather stitch one side, remove quilt from machine, clip threads, then stitch the next side. This stitching will stabilize the edge of the quilt top, batting and backing and eliminate stretching during quilting.

Warning: Some of these stitches will need to be removed during quilting in order to avoid quilting a pucker near the quilt top's edge. That's OK.

In-the-ditch Quilting

I'm a big believer in in-the-ditch quilting. I love how it keeps straight seams straight along blocks and borders and keeps curves neatly in place. It also makes applique and other elements pop!

Ditch stitching should be on the low side of the seam, in the shadow. The low side is the side without a seam allowance. When stitching the low side of the ditch, sometimes it will be on the right, and sometimes on the left. Where rows are joined, for instance, and seams are butted up, the low side/seam allowances switch directions. It's really no problem.

Avoid quilting in the ditch of seams pressed open. Stitching would be over threads only and not through fabric. For this reason, I only press open very short seams where no quilting is required.

Placing a hand on each side of the seam can help guide the quilt through the machine straight. I sometimes use my hands to part the fabrics allowing the needle to get in the ditch. I'm careful not to pull more with one hand than the other. The seam should remain straight. If the seam is not straight, I pull more with one hand than the other to straighten it.

After preparing the quilt sandwich, ditch quilt border seams taking great care to keep seams straight, then ditch sashing and around blocks. Finally, quilt around major motifs or features. After quilting ditches, nearly all safety pins have been removed so fewer obstacles are encountered during decorative quilting.

Intermittent pressing during quilting can straighten seams if they begin to distort and can flatten the quilt, making it easier to manage in the sewing machine. I like 100% cotton and 100% wool battings. When I use a wool batting, I smash a section at a time with heat and steam just before quilting. This reduces the chance of shifting and makes each section smaller and easier to fit into the machine. Wool poofs up later to fill open areas.

The right tools can help. My favorites are:

• A sewing machine with great **speed control**. Many now have sliders or buttons to control the machine's speed and it's wise to take advantage of such an option.

• An **open-toe foot walking foot**, or better yet a **built-in walking foot with an open-toe** makes seeing the needle go up and down into the seam (or beside an applique) much easier.

• The **Needle positioning** feature is a great help. I find moving the needle to the right a bit helps me guide the seam through the machine straighter. I use the inside edge of the foot as a guide for keeping seams approaching the needle straight (not at an angle).

• A sewing machine built into a table or with a surround makes it easier to flatten bigger portions of the quilt.

• Of course, **thin thread** is beneficial as this stitching is never ever to be seen. See *"Thin Threads"* on page 7. With any of these, I have great success with a 50wt or 60wt cotton (regular piecing thread) in the bobbin. Thread color also matters. Choose a color to match or one that is slightly darker than one of the fabrics on either side of the ditch.

• **Needles** can make a difference as well. I prefer a 60/8 Microtex needle and if my thread suffers in such a tiny needle, I use a 70/10 Jeans or 70/10 Microtex. When stitching in that tiny ditch, a larger needle feels like eating my morning cereal with a garden spade (not that I've actually done that).

• A **stitch length** of 2.0mm seems to be just right for hiding down in the shadows. Bigger stitches allow thread to lay on top of the fabric and smaller stitches are difficult to keep straight. You may need to experiment with your machine to determine your ideal in-the-ditch stitch length.

• Many quilters find that holding a pointy tool in the ditch just ahead of the needle while stitching is extremely helpful. I recommend the **Clover Ball Point Awl** for this task as it's pointy enough to get into the ditch, but is not sharp enough to tear or damage fabric.

DO NOT DITCH SEAMS WHICH ARE PRESSED OPEN (SUCH AS THESE SHORT SEAMS BETWEEN TRIANGLES)

Decorative Quilting ~ machine

I'll confess. For a long time I felt insufficient when it came to decorative quilting. My free-motion skills are stinky and my brain doesn't work that way. I learned this early on and found I needed another way to add decorative quilting to my work.

Ah-ha! The wonderful world of heavy decorative threads is my answer. I can quilt simple designs with my feed dogs up and let the beautiful thread do the work!

Marking quilting designs is easy with **freezer paper templates**. Pre-shrink freezer paper, draw quilting designs on the paper side, cut out design, press to quilt with dry iron (shiny side down), and stitch beside paper. Re-use paper again and again.

Freezer paper in 8.5"x 11" sheets can run through an inkjet printer. Draw quilting designs on the computer and print on these sheets to avoid the need for tracing.

Quilting around appliquéed motifs with a heavy decorative thread adds impact and a certain glow to the piece as in *Hippie Daisies* on page 107.

For wonderful thread choices and other info, please see *"Heavy Decorative Threads"* on page 6 and *"Stitching Heavy Threads"* on page 34.

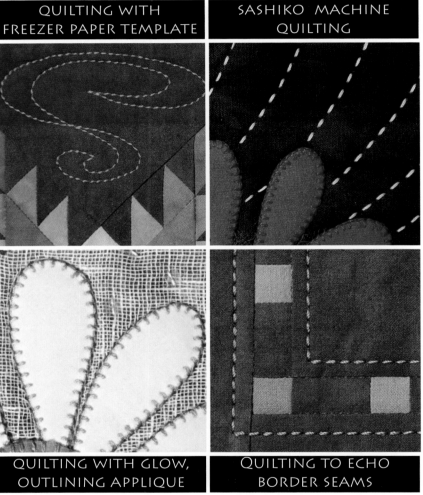

QUILTING WITH FREEZER PAPER TEMPLATE

SASHIKO MACHINE QUILTING

QUILTING WITH GLOW, OUTLINING APPLIQUE

QUILTING TO ECHO BORDER SEAMS

Beginning and Ending ~ machine

Heavy threads look best with big stitches (3–3.5mm) and when a stitching line comes back to its beginning, sometimes the last stitch is smaller than the others. In order to hide this, I suggest beginning to stitch in a seam line or quilting intersection. This will make that last stitch's length less conspicuous.

Many quilters begin and end machine quilting with miniscule stitches so that threads do not need to be tied off, and they are clipped at the quilt's surface. When this is done with heavy decorative threads, a "thread booger" is formed. Judges will frown on this "embellishment" every time.

I avoid this unsightly mess by leaving thread tails at the beginning and end of every stitching line. I then pull threads to the wrong side of the quilt, tie top and bobbin threads together, and bury the knot and tails in the quilt's batting.

To bury the knot, thread all threads into a tapestry needle, enter quilt backing in the same hole threads are coming out, exit backing about 1" away. Pull needle to pop knot through backing then trim threads at quilt's surface.

Choosing a backing fabric that I enjoy very much is of utmost importance given the time I spend tie-ing knots and burying thread tails. So, give some thought to your backing fabric choice. Choosing a fabric that is not too densely woven will make it easier to pop the knot, and a busy print will help hide the little bulge of the knot.

I use a tapestry needle (size 24–26) or Spiral Eye™ Side Threading Needle (size SE-4) to bury knots and thread tails. The Spiral Eye™ is much gentler on threads than a traditional self-threading needle.

I begin and end *all* machine quilting lines (thin threads or heavy threads) by pulling threads to the back tying off, and burying knots/tails. Make your own beginning/ending choice. I, obviously, need to get a life.

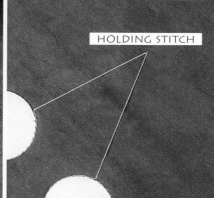

STITCH BESIDE FREEZER PAPER WITH OPEN-TOE

FREEZER PAPER

When jumping from one area of quilting to another it's usually not necessary to pull the whole quilt out of the machine, clip threads and begin again. Sometimes it's possible to end one stitching line and begin again at another point without pulling the quilt out of the machine and clipping threads.

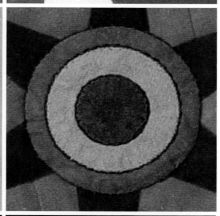

PULL THREADS TO BACK, TIE, BURY KNOT/TAILS

When ending and beginning points are close together, I prefer to come to the end of a stitching line and place a holding stitch a few inches away from my ending point and a few inches away from my next beginning point. Later, I'll pull the top thread,

clip both threads and I have enough tail at each end to tie off.

Traditionally, the beginning bobbin thread tail is pulled to the top of the quilt after a couple of stitches. Since my quilting designs are simple, I leave the bobbin tail on the wrong side of the quilt during quilting. After a few stitches, I pull the **top thread to the back** (making sure tails are not in my path). After every 20 minutes or so, I stop quilting to pull all top threads to the wrong side, tie knots and burry tails. *Of course, this is only successful if quilting lines don't cross over each other to tangle tails.*

HOLDING STITCH

HOLDING STITCH

THIN THREAD APPLIQUE, QUILTED WITH HEAVY

Sashiko by Machine

Do yourself a big favor and check out the Sashiko® machine by Baby Lock®. It replicates the look of hand quilting—with a space between every stitch. Each stitch is composed of two threads. You have to see it to believe it.

While documentation that comes with the machine suggests using threads of 30wt and smaller, I have tremendous success with WonderFil Spagetti 12wt cotton. Loosening the bobbin tension a tiny bit and stitching slowly is essential. I think this machine is magic. Please see *Japanese Daisies* on page 60.

Quilting by Hand with Heavy Decorative Threads

The texture and, well, hand-made look of hand quilting is charming. Hand quilting with heavy decorative threads is quick and rewarding. It's great for beginners, too, because the big stitches we make as beginning hand quilters are perfectly appropriate for heavy threads.

I haven't the space to go into great detail on hand quilting, but here are suggestions to get you started.

Marking quilting designs can be challenging. Freezer paper templates don't work well when the quilt is manipulated for hand stitching. Masking tape is great for straight lines. A Hera marker (or corner of a credit card) can be dragged along the quilt to leave an indentation for quilting lines. All markers must be tested before use.

CONFETTI QUILTING

MORSE CODE QUILTING
2 STRANDS SPAGETTI 12WT

HAND QUILTING WITH #8 PEARL COTTON

2 EXIT HERE

1 INSERT NEEDLE HERE AND TUNNEL

3. STITCH OVER TUNNELED THREAD TO PIERCE IT

For thread candidates, please see *"Heavy Decorative Threads"* on page 6. Double a 12wt thread for more impact as in *Hippie Daisies* on page 107.

Size 7 or 8 between needles are wonderful for these threads but don't try using a needle threader ... especially your friend's needle threader. It will break.

I strongly recommend using a finger cot for any hand sewing. See *"Finger Cots"* on page 8.

A thimble with deep dimples is a must to push the needle through layers of a quilt. Many styles and brands are available.

Quilt in a hoop, frame, or on your lap (hoop-less), whatever is most comfortable for you.

Stitch length is personal preference. I seem to like about 4–5 stitches to the inch. (A stitch is one "over" and one "under".)

To thread the needle, cut a fresh end, bite the end to wet and flatten it, pinch thread end between thumb and forefinger, peel back fingers to barely expose end, then bring needle to thread. Needle holes are stamped and sometimes one side of the hole is smoother than the other, so it might be helpful to turn the needle if one way isn't working.

Thread the entire package of needles onto the spool before stitching, while your eyes are fresh. When it's time to stitch, pull off a length of thread with only one needle on it, pushing extra needles toward the spool. Cut a length of thread with only one needle on it. It's embarrassing to cut the length with all the needles on it or with no needles even if you're the only one at home when it happens. So don't do that.

Beginning and ending needs some attention as it's undesirable to pop a knot through your wonderful fabric when even a single knot with heavy thread is kind of big. There are times it is necessary, but there are options.

Piercing the thread is one beginning option. Tunnel under the beginning quilting path and quilt over the tunneled thread to pierce it. This is surprisingly secure.

Weaving a beginning or ending tail is a slick trick. All weaving is done within the quilt sandwich, between quilt top and backing.

To weave a beginning tail, leave a 5″ tail at the beginning of the quilting line.

1. At the beginning or end of a quilting line, place the needle into the quilt top pointing toward stitches. Weave back and forth to the right and left of stitches.

2. Pull needle part-way out, turn around and push the point to weave another needle length.

3. Turn needle and park it in fabric. Pull extra thread through.

4. Pull needle part-way out and wiggle back and forth one needle length toward the end of the stitching line. Pull needle all the way out and clip thread at quilt's surface.

1. WEAVE OUT ONE NEEDLE LENGTH	3. PARK NEEDLE TO PULL THREAD THROUGH
2. WEAVE AWAY ANOTHER NEEDLE LENGTH	4. COME BACK ONE NEEDLE LENGTH

Hand Stitching Alternatives

Stitching a dashed line is not the only hand stitching option. Lots of fabulous texture can be achieved with hand stitching. I love it! If you do too, visit Laura Wasilowski's Artfabrik web page for tips on threads and stitching by hand. Please see *"Resources"* on page 110.

Rambling seed stitches make great quilting designs. I prefer to stitch each "seed" twice through all layers, then tunnel under the quilt top to the next stitch. This is one case where I can do *random* and thoroughly enjoy it. (Rambling has never been a problem for me.) See *Party Star* on page 104 and previous page. I call it **confetti quilting**.

Scattering X's over a quilt's surface is fun too. Once again, I go over each stitch twice through all layers and then tunnel just under the quilt top to the next X.

I have a new favorite! I've dubbed it **Morse Code Quilting**. Take several traditional hand quilting stitches and randomly insert French knots. See *Hippie Daisies* on page 107 and previous page. The quilting looks rather like a beaded curtain, don't you think? Peace, baby!

Embellishing

Quilters are treated to an ever-growing array of wonderful embellishments, so keep looking for more. Quilts in this publication feature embellishments of beads, sequins, buttons, silk ribbon, felted wool, ric-rac, and sheer fabrics. Be still my heart.

I'm often asked if embellishments are to be added before or after quilting. For two reasons, I prefer to add embellishments during or after quilting. If they are sewn to the quilt top prior to quilting, they could get in the way during quilting or worse yet, they could get caught on the sewing machine or in a quilting hoop and damage fabric. The other reason I like adding embellishments during or after quilting is that I like the look of the embellishment

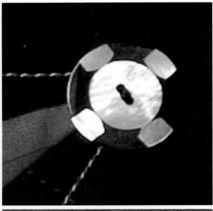

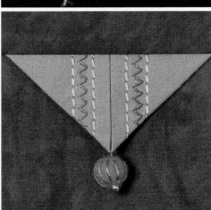

pulled into the quilt sandwich a bit. They appear more secure that way. Of course, there are exceptions to every "rule", so use your own judgement, but take these concerns into consideration.

Embellishments may be added as quilting to fill background areas. Selecting quilting designs sometimes baffles me but scattering beads in a background is quite entertaining. Stitch through the quilt sandwich and pass through each bead at least twice, then tunnel through batting to the next location.

Using embellishments as major design elements is particularly fun. Borders and/or star point tips love to be embellished. They speak to me, yes.

I'm positively giddy while sewing beads or felted wool balls to the tips of prairie points. (not kidding)

Please don't feel you need to be an expert beader or embellisher to add precious doo-dads to your work. Be sure the item will not damage your fabric, then have at it. I test to be sure items can withstand the punishment of steam and extreme heat without breaking or bleeding color before I use them, and I suggest you do the same. Nymo, Silamide and FireLine are threads on the market specifically for beading, but I sometimes stitch with regular cotton thread matching the embellishment or fabric. Cotton thread may only be used with embellishments that are very smooth or soft and will not cut thread. I use whatever needle will go through my embellishment.

When sewing items to your quilt, securing knots is very important. Knots must be secure and neat. It's OK to pop a knot through backing fabric, but then add a backstitch to reduce stress on that knot.

The traditional ending knot (backstitch, then pass needle/thread through loop twice and pull) may be used at the beginning or end. Thread tails must be hidden. Sometimes it's easier to hide a knot under the embellishment.

Beads may be added to prairie points (PPs) in two ways: dangling or sewn through the quilt. In either case, thread should be passed through fabric and beads twice.

• To sew dangling beads, hide knots inside the PP. This is more easily done before it is sewn into a seam.

• An easier alternative is to sew beads onto the PP during quilting and stitch through all layers. Knots may be hidden under the quilt backing.

Opposite page (clock-wise from top left):

• Organza with frayed edges under applique, quilted with pearl and glass beads

• Button as accent at star tip and *Twisted Thread Illusion*, see page 35

• Embellished prairie point with dangling embellished felted wool ball

• Embellished appliqueed circle: silk ribbon asterisk and heavy silk thread stitched onto fabric before invisible machine applique

This page (clock-wise from top left):

• Felted wool ball cut in half and embellished with silk ribbon and glass bead, stitched on to quilt with a giant asterisk passing through center of ball

• Embellished prairie points with wood and glass beads at tips, stitching with WonderFil Spagetti 12wt cotton in the Baby Lock Sashiko machine

• Square sequins as quilting over linen gauze

• Embellished prairie points with felted wool balls and glass beads at tips

• Wood and glass beads as accents in border

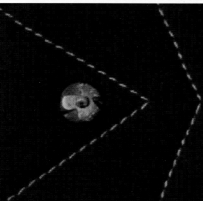

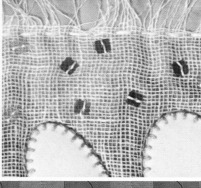
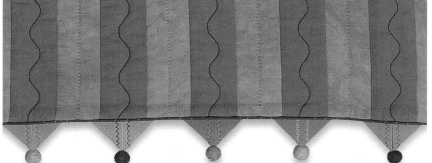

Stitching with heavy decorative threads is great fun and offers spectacular results with just a little practice. I suggest stitching with heavy decorative threads to applique, embellish prairie points, embellish fabric before it is cut, and as quilting through all layers of a quilt.

The "#" or "wt" (weight) listed on a thread spool is only a guideline as to its size … like shoe sizes. You don't march into the shoe shop and expect every same-size shoe to fit the same, do you? Generally, the higher the number, the smaller the thread. Larger numbers denote smaller threads. Oh, good gracious, how are we to keep it all straight? For example, a #100 thread is very fine and a 3wt pearl cotton is quite heavy. I prefer heavy threads from 30wt to 12wt.

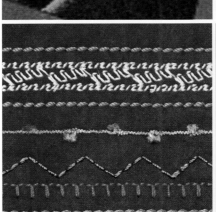
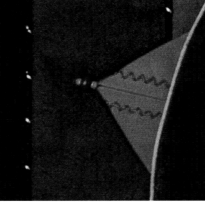
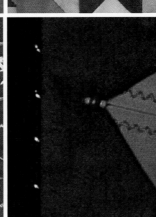

a smaller hole but if it doesn't yield good stitches, I use the 100/16 topstitch needle.

Topstitch needles are special. They have a large eye to accommodate heavy thread. A wealth of information is available at www.Schmetzneedles.com. I was not previously aware that every sewing machine needle has a butt.

Bobbin thread ~ Use regular (50 or 60wt) cotton thread in the bobbin. For best results, wind the bobbin on your machine. Don't use a separate bobbin winder, or a pre-wound bobbin. Your machine's bobbin winder will put proper tension on thread as it is wound.

Different bobbin thread colors will give different results. Experiment with matching top thread color, matching fabric color, or choosing something completely different. A bobbin thread slightly darker than the top thread will accentuate the definition of each stitch.

Machine Stitching

Please see *"Heavy Decorative Threads"* on page 6 and *"Resources"* on page 110 for information on the plethora of threads available to us.

Needles ~ Use a 100/16 topstitch needle in the machine. I prefer using a 90/14 topstitch needle to poke

Starch fabrics. Large needles require fabric with some body so fabric isn't pushed down into the needle plate. When quilting through the layers of a quilt, this is not an issue.

Simple stitches are best for heavy threads. Intricate designs are better suited to finer threads. Please don't underestimate the beauty of a zig-zag or straight stitch. I prefer straight stitches 3–4mm in length to show off heavy decorative threads.

Practice on a sample to adjust stitch length, width, and tension to your liking. If the decorative thread is tight on the fabric's surface rather than pulled down into the fabric, the top tension needs to be loosened. A lower number is less tension.

Starting/stopping ~ If stitching through stabilized fabric only (not the layers of a quilt), simply pull threads to the wrong side and knot and/or dot with permanent fabric glue. If stitching through layers of a quilt, see *"Beginning and Ending"* on page 28.

Trouble-shooting ~ machine

If problems arise, try these remedies (one at a time).

• Re-thread the machine.

• Re-seat the bobbin.

• Adjust top tension.

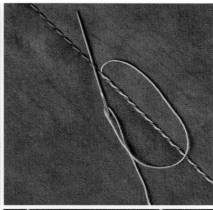

• Replace the needle and/or try a 100/16 topstitch if the 90/14 topstitch isn't giving good results. Sometimes a brand new needle is faulty, so try another.

• Try a simple straight stitch with the needle in the center needle position and a stitch length of 3.5mm. If this stitch is great, but others are not, your machine may need service.

• Try a different bobbin. Sometimes a bobbin isn't wound well or has a burr which causes problems. A very full or nearly empty bobbin can affect tension.

• Move the spool from a vertical spindle to a horizontal spindle or vice versa. Change the spool end for end. Some quilters report best success using a separate thread stand.

• Leave the machine, pet the dog, have a nap, then drink a latte. Everything will seem better.

Hand Quilting

Hand quilting with heavy threads is very rewarding!

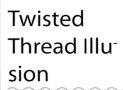

Larger stitches are appropriate, so the task is quick. See *"Quilting by Hand with Heavy Decorative Threads"* on page 30.

Twisted Thread Illusion

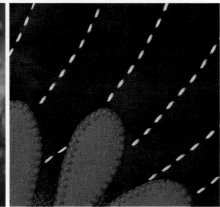

This is my favorite thread trick! Please see *Kauai Chicken Star* on the cover and page 89, *Bouncin'* on page 100, and *Twirling Tassels* on page 103.

First, quilt by machine with heavy decorative thread and large, 3.5mm, stitches.

Thread another color of the same weight thread into a tapestry needle (size 24–26). By hand, whip the new color under every machine-made stitch to create the twisted thread illusion. TaDa! It's easy, fun and you didn't have anything better to do anyway!

Formerly cutesy pie and sickeningly sweet, prairie points can now be striking, elegant and all around maah-velous, dahling! Of course, there are times cutie-tootie is appropriate too.

Use fabric texture, color, and embellishments

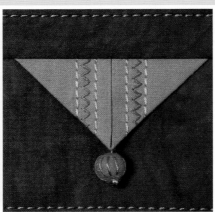

to create the style your work deserves. Slip these little pieces of preciousness anywhere: in seams, in binding, in piped curves, or in piped bindings. They can be major design elements or subtle accents — whatever your heart desires.

Prairie Points: plain/embellished

Embellished prairie points are featured in projects *Trio* on page 77, *Happy Daisy* on page 67, *Japanese Daisies* on page 61, *Kauai Chicken Star* on page 89 and *Prairie Point Pillow* on page 83.

• Starch fabric.

• Cut strips. Choose prairie point (PP) finished height to determine size to cut strip(s). Use chart or add seam allowance to PP FINISHED HEIGHT and double.

• Press strips in half lengthwise, wrong sides together.

• For embellished PPs, add decorative stitching near fold. Please see "Stitching Heavy Threads" on page 34.

• Cut into segments same length as strip cut width (not folded).

• On pressing surface, place folded segments right side down with folds away from you. (If there's no decorative stitching, there's no right side.)

Prairie point finished height	Cut strip width/ cut segment length
½"	1½"
¾"	2"
1"	2½"
1¼"	3"
1½"	3½"
1¾"	4"
2"	4½"
2¼"	5"
2½"	5½"

Cut strip width based on ¼" seam allowance.
To determine other "cut strip widths":
(PP FINISHED HEIGHT + SEAM ALLOWANCE) X 2 = CUT STRIP WIDTH

- Place Prairie Pointer tool over segment aligning appropriate line on tool with cut edges of segment. Use line corresponding with segment length.

- Fold top corners over tool to meet at center line.

- Carefully place iron over PP/tool, remove fingers from fabric and slide tool out of PP immediately (before tool gets hot). Do not remove iron.

- Hold iron in place and steam if desired then remove iron to reveal perfect prairie point!

- Continue to make more PPs using cool areas of pressing surface.

Note: If you're not using the Prairie Pointer tool, bring 2 top corners to bottom center and press. Be careful to align all cut edges and avoid a pucker at the point.

| PLACE PP RIGHT SIDE DOWN, PLACE TOOL OVER | BRING CORNERS TO CENTER, PRESS, REMOVE TOOL | SLIDE TOOL OUT |

Tip: To dangle beads from prairie point, hide knots inside the PP and pass through PP and beads twice. This is more easily done before PPs are sewn into a seam.

Tip: Another option is to stitch beads during quilting which involves stitching through the PP's tip and all layers of the quilt. They don't dangle with this option. Pass needle and thread through beads and quilt at least twice.

Prairie Points: lined

Lined prairie points are featured in the project *Octet* on page 71.

- Choose two fabrics, main and lining (strip in center of PP), starch then cut strips according to chart. Lining strip is cut ½" wider than main strip.

- Sew main and lining together with ¼" seam allowance. Press seam allowance toward main.

- Press pieced strip in half with wrong sides together.

- Add stitching if desired. See *"Stitching Heavy Threads"* on page 34.

- Cut into segments according to chart.

- Press into prairie points as described above. Right side of PP is side with both fabrics showing.

Prairie point finished height	Cut lining strip width	Cut main strip width	Cut segment length
1"	1¾"	1¼"	2½"
1½"	2¼"	1¾"	3½"
2"	2¾"	2¼"	4½"
2½"	3¼"	2¾"	5½"

Cut strip width based on ¼" seam allowance.
Use line on Prairie Pointer tool corresponding to "cut segment length".

Binding

Prepare Quilt

These instructions are for a double-fold plain binding with mitered corners.

• Quilt the quilt. Please see *"Preparing the Quilt Sandwich"* on page 26 to find tips on stay-stitching the quilt's edge and quilting.

• A quilt's edges do not stay straight during quilting, so the quilt must be squared up before binding is applied. Square up quilt by **drawing a new edge**. Measure from border seams to determine where to place these lines. (These lines will end up deep into the fold of the binding at the very outside edge of the quilt.) *Don't cut excess at this time!*

> *Tip: Keeping excess quilt top/batting/backing on the quilt will protect the edge from stretching. Excess may be cut after binding has been sewn to secure the edge.*
>
> *When adding piping at a quilt's edge, I cut the excess after the piping has been sewn to the quilt to secure the edge. The bottom line is, I don't cut excess until something has been sewn along the quilt's edge to secure it.*

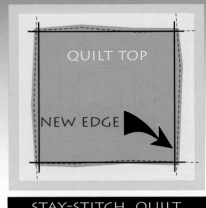

STAY-STITCH, QUILT, DRAW NEW EDGE

Prepare Binding

• Measure around quilt and cut enough 2¼″ strips to go around quilt plus at least 10″ extra. Straight of grain is fine for straight edges, but bias is required for curvy edges. Please note, bias washes and wears better, even on straight edges.

• Make one long strip by splicing strips together with diagonal seams as shown. Allow extra length to extend beyond fabric overlap. Angles at ends of strips don't matter (straight or diagonal). Use a tiny, 1.5mm stitch length, press seams open, then trim seam allowances to about ¼″.

• Press long strip wrong sides together lengthwise.

• Cut ends of binding perpendicular to fold, removing any selvage or angled end.

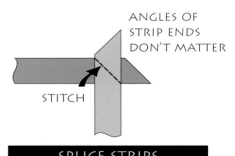

ANGLES OF STRIP ENDS DON'T MATTER

STITCH

SPLICE STRIPS

PRESS STRIPS

Apply Binding

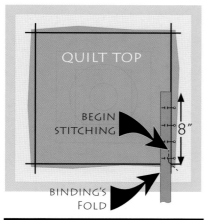

PLACE BINDING ALONG NEW EDGE, SEW

• Lay folded binding on quilt aligning cut edges of binding with **new edge** as shown. End of tail should be about 8″ ahead of corner. Pin in place

• Leave about 6″ of unsewn tail behind machine and begin stitching about 2″ from corner of quilt with ¼″ seam allowance. Stop ¼″ before next **new edge**. Lock end of stitching line by either backstitching or by turning and sewing off corner of quilt.

• Remove quilt from machine and clip threads.

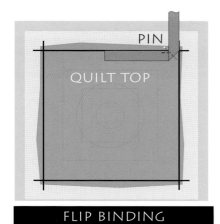

FLIP BINDING AWAY FROM NEXT EDGE

• To miter corner, turn quilt counter clockwise one quarter turn as shown. Flip binding up and away from next edge. Next **new edge** and cut edge of binding must be in a straight line. Pin binding.

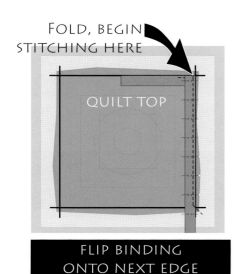

FLIP BINDING ONTO NEXT EDGE

• Fold binding along next **new edge** making sure binding's fold is directly over previous **new edge**. The placement of this fold determines if the corner of the binding will be square, rounded, or too pointy.

• Begin stitching with a ¼″ seam allowance at quilt's **new edge** and stop ¼″ before next **new edge** as done previously. Lock end of stitching by either backstitching or by turning and sewing off corner of quilt.

• Repeat for each corner/side, but after last corner, stop stitching at least 8″ before beginning stitching point. There must be at least an 8″ gap to join tails.

Join Tails

- Lay tails on top of one another and cut ending tail so it overlaps beginning tail "binding cut width plus ¼". For binding cut 2¼", overlap should be 2½".

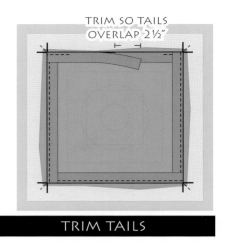

TRIM TAILS

- KISS: Unfold tails, place right sides together matching ends. Fold quilt if necessary.

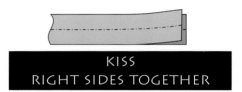

KISS
RIGHT SIDES TOGETHER

- TWIST: Turn one tail 90 degrees, so tails make the corner of a square. If this is awkward because too much tail is attached to the quilt, remove some binding stitches so there is more loose tail to work with. It may be necessary to fold the quilt at this point.

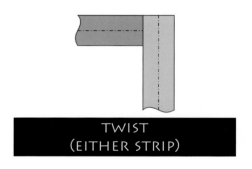

TWIST
(EITHER STRIP)

- WIGGLE: Slide each tail so ⅛" sticks out beyond the other tail. Don't be skimpy with the ⅛". Pin in place.

- Sew diagonal seam as shown from crevasse to crevasse with small stitches and finger press seam open. Before trimming seam allowance, test the length of binding by folding binding and laying it along the quilt's edge, when you see that it is correct, trim seam allowance to about ¼".

- Finish machine sewing binding to quilt.

- Trim excess quilt top/batting/backing along binding's cut edge. *Be careful at corners to avoid cutting into binding's fold near corners.*

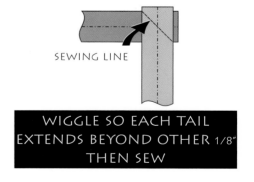

WIGGLE SO EACH TAIL
EXTENDS BEYOND OTHER 1/8"
THEN SEW

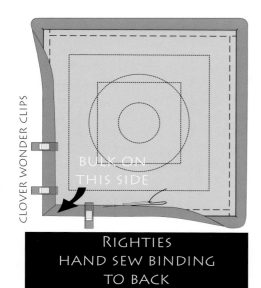

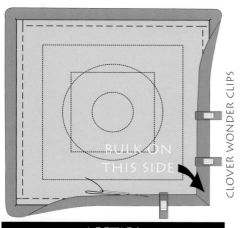

Finish Back

• Wrap binding to back of quilt so the binding is full of backing/batting/quilt top and hand stitch in place. Binding will wrap beyond stitching lines and that's OK. This makes corners easier to deal with. If you prefer less binding on the back, cut a 2″-wide strip. Do everything else the same but recalculate tail overlap.

• At corners, fold bulk on back opposite bulk on front.

• Many judges will check to see that binding is stitched down at the mitered corners. While I always do this on the back miter, I stitch front miters on show quilts only.

Optional Wide Binding

Much of the time I prefer a wide binding. For a wide binding (about ⅝″ finished), more must be done than simply cutting wider binding strips. Since it's important to stuff binding all the way to the outermost fold, a wider seam allowance must be taken.

• Cut binding strips 3½″ wide.

• Draw **new edge**. Keep in mind more of the outer border will be caught in binding seam. Make sure that's OK for this quilt.

• Use ½″ seam allowance to sew binding to quilt.

• Stop stitching ½″ before next **new edge** rather than ¼″.

• When cutting ending tail, overlap should be 3¾″ (binding cut width plus ¼″).

Optional Machine Finish

If you prefer a machine finish, first press binding away from seam on right side of quilt, then flip quilt over and press binding around to back. Press miters in corners taking care that bulk on back is on opposite side of bulk on front. Use a thin strip of fusible web to hold binding in place, then flip quilt to right side and machine stitch on quilt beside binding. Binding on back will be caught in stitching line. This is not a show-quality finish, but it is secure.

Piped Bindings

See "Resources" on page 110 for information on *Piping Hot Binding.*

Niners
Susan K Cleveland
20"x 15½", 2003

Niners

There's something about a nine-patch I just love and this one is all dressed up with a skinny border and heavy decorative threads. Of course, more could be added, but this seemed just right for these fabrics.

I hope you enjoy practicing precision piecing and learning some tricks with skinny borders on this project.

Fabric	Needed	Sample	Yours	Cut
background	1yd	navy hand-dyed		*cut on lengthwise grain, see page 11, strips will be ~36"* (~ means approximately) • cut (4) 2½" strips, label (2) **inner borders,** label (2) **outer borders** • cut (3) 1½" strips • then cut those 1½" strips into » (6) ~6" pieces, label **blocks** » (6) exact 1½" squares, label **blocks** » (14) 3½" rectangles, label **pieced border** • from remaining yardage, cut » 22"x 19" piece for backing » (3) strips for binding your desired width » (2) 3½" squares, label **blocks** » (2) 5½" squares, cut an X (twice diagonally), label **sides** » (2) 3" squares, cut once diagonally, label **corners**
features	(6) 3"x 17" strips	orange/ gold/pink/ green/ red/blue hand-dyes		from each of (6) fabrics cut: • (1) 1½"x at least 17" piece » then cut each into ~4", ~6", and (2) 3½" segments • choose one feature for corners of pieced border and cut (2) 1"x 3½" pieces, label **pieced border corners**
backing & batting	fat quarter			22"x 19"
binding	fat quarter	navy		as desired

decorative thread for quilting
piping fabric: fat quarter; 1/16" cording: 3yds (optional)
freezer paper for quilting templates

Fabric requirements are based on fabrics 40"–44" in width.
A fat quarter measures approximately 18"x 20" and a fat eighth approximately 9"x 22".
Starch all fabrics before cutting.
All seam allowances are ¼".
Piped binding instructions are written in great detail in Piping Hot Binding. Please see "Resources" on page 110.

Trim Setting Triangles

Trimming setting triangles makes building rows and assembling the quilt body much easier and more precise, so it's well worth the time.

• Carefully trim background triangles labeled *sides* 3½" wide, then flip over (wrong side up and repeat). Make 6. There will be 2 extra.

• Carefully trim background triangles labeled *corners* 1¾" from center tip, then flip over (wrong side up and repeat). Make 4.

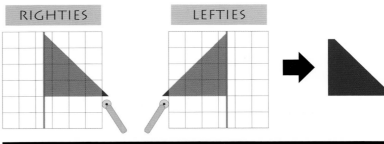

TRIM SIDE SETTING TRIANGLES 3½" WIDE
FLIP OVER TO TRIM OTHER CORNER

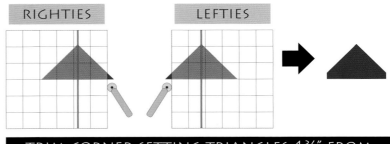

TRIM CORNER SETTING TRIANGLES 1¾" FROM
CENTER, FLIP OVER TO TRIM OTHER CORNER

Build Nine-patch Blocks

Repeat these steps for each feature fabric. Note pressing directions as they will make segments fit together nicely if followed.

Use background pieces labeled *blocks* and *features* measuring 1½"x ~4" and 1½"x ~6". Take care to choose the correct pieces.

• Sew ~6" background strip to ~6" feature strip and press seam allowance toward feature.

• Sew ~4" feature strip to background strip and press seam allowance toward feature.

• From this strip set, cut (2) 1½" segments from 3-strip portion.

• From 2-strip portion, cut (1) 1½" segment.

• Add 1½" background square to segment of 2-strip portion and press toward feature.

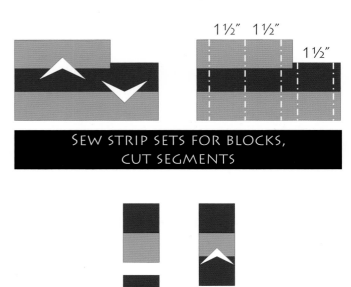

SEW STRIP SETS FOR BLOCKS,
CUT SEGMENTS

FINISH CENTER SEGMENT

ASSEMBLE 9-PATCH BLOCKS

• Assemble 9-patch blocks as shown pressing toward center unit. Blocks should measure 3½″ square.

Assemble Quilt Body

• Arrange nine-patch blocks, plain 3½″ blocks, and backgrounds labeled *sides* and *corners* as shown.

• Sew rows, noting pressing directions so seams will nest when rows are joined.

• Sew rows together noting pressing directions.

ASSEMBLE ROWS

Tip: Use the Wacker tool to flatten bulky seam allowances (and release pent up emotions). A flat quilt is much easier to quilt and looks so nice.

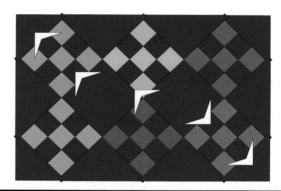

ASSEMBLE QUILT BODY

BUILD PIECED BORDER STRIP SETS

Build Pieced Border Strip Sets

Each pieced border strip set will be used twice. See *"Skinny Pieced Borders"* on page 24 for details or read ahead if the suspense is eating you up.

• Collect (14) 1½″x 3½″ backgrounds labeled *pieced border* and (12) feature pieces labeled *pieced border*.

• Arrange as you like alternating backgrounds and features taking into account which feature was chosen as *pieced border corners*.

• Piece as shown, using a 1.5mm stitch length. Press all seam allowances open.

Inner Border

} Tip: Since piecing is rarely perfect, it's best to piece borders, then adjust either the border or body of quilt to fit perfectly.

There are two ways to handle a border between the quilt body and pieced border. One way is to calculate the *filler* needed between the actual quilt body and pieced border, and another way is to add an inner border that is wider than needed, then trim the quilt body with inner border to match the pieced border. I prefer to add a wide border and trim to accurately fit the pieced border.

• Measure width of quilt body, and cut (2) *inner border* pieces this length.

• Sew to top and bottom of quilt body and press seam allowances toward borders.

• Measure new length of quilt body, and cut (2) *inner border* pieces this length.

• Sew to sides of quilt body and press seam allowances toward borders.

• Trim quilt to match pieced border sizes. Measure pieced border lengths and trim quilt making sure to keep blocks centered. *Do not lay border over quilt and trim along ends of pieced borders as this is not accurate.*

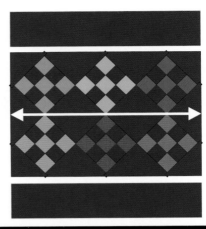

MEASURE WIDTH OF QUILT BODY, CUT TOP/BOTTOM INNER BORDERS, SEW

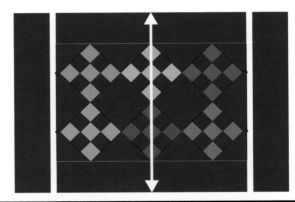

MEASURE LENGTH OF QUILT BODY, CUT SIDE INNER BORDERS, SEW

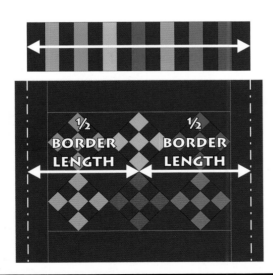

TRIM QUILT BODY WIDTH TO MATCH LONG PIECED BORDER

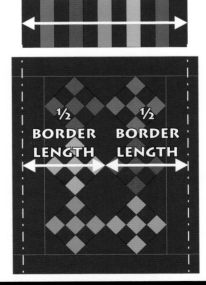

TRIM QUILT BODY LENGTH TO MATCH SHORT PIECED BORDER

Pieced Border

Tip: Each pieced border strip set will be added to the quilt, then trimmed to correct width. This eliminates the pieced border's tendency to stretch.

• Add corner pieces to short border strip set. Stitch with 1.5mm stitches and press seam allowances toward corner pieces so seam allowances nest when border is sewn to quilt body.

• Trim one edge of each pieced border strip set to make a clean, straight edge on each strip set. Check to be sure seams are parallel to lines on the ruler. (This clean, straight edge will be sewn to the quilt.)

• Sew long pieced border to top of quilt body, press seam allowances toward plain border, then trim pieced border ¾" away from seam.

• Repeat with remaining long pieced border at bottom of quilt.

• Sew short pieced border to one side of quilt body, matching seams along corner pieces. Press seam allowances toward plain border, then trim pieced border ¾" away from seam.

• Repeat with remaining short pieced border at other side of quilt.

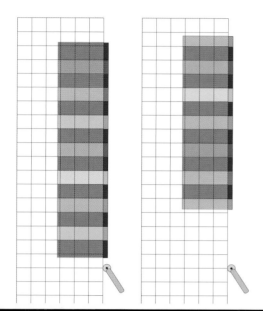

TRIM LONG EDGE OF EACH
PIECED BORDER STRIP SET

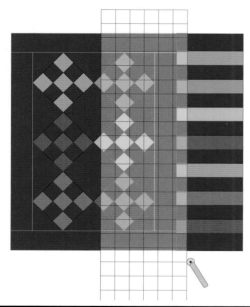

ADD PIECED BORDER STRIP SET TO
TOP OF QUILT, PRESS, TRIM ¾" FROM SEAM
THEN REPEAT FOR BOTTOM

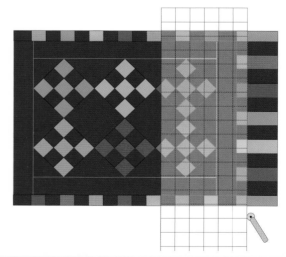

ADD PIECED BORDER STRIP SET TO
SIDE OF QUILT, PRESS, TRIM ¾" FROM SEAM
THEN REPEAT FOR OTHER SIDE

Add Outer Border

• Measure width of quilt then cut two outer border pieces this length. These strips were cut earlier but were not cut to length.

• Sew outer border pieces to top and bottom of quilt pressing seam allowances toward outer border.

• Measure new length of quilt and cut two outer border pieces this length. These strips were cut earlier but were not cut to length.

• Sew outer border pieces to sides of quilt pressing seam allowances toward outer border.

Quilt & Embellish

• Layer quilt top, batting and backing. Press so layers cling together. Pin layers together and stitch with long stitch length through all layers near each edge of quilt top. This stitching will protect edges from stretching during quilting.

• I suggest using a thin silk or cotton thread to quilt in the ditch of border seams and around each block. Do not ditch quilt seams that are pressed open.

• For decorative quilting I used WonderFil Spagetti 12wt cotton thread.

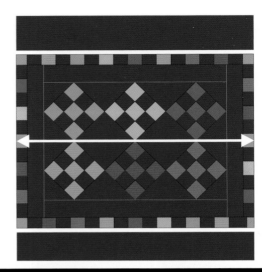

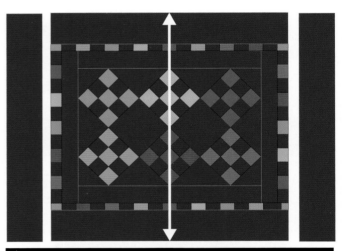

OUTER BORDER:
MEASURE, CUT TO LENGTH, SEW

OUTER BORDER:
MEASURE, CUT TO LENGTH, SEW

Finish

• Draw quilt's new edge 2″ from outer border seam. Binding or piping will be placed along this new edge.

• For binding instructions, please see *"Binding"* on page 38 or refer to *Piping Hot Binding*, a booklet containing very detailed instructions for finishing quilts with a beautiful piped binding.

• Label your quilt.

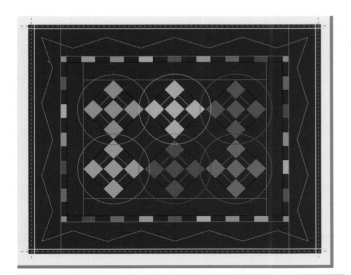

LAYER, STAY-STITCH, QUILT,
DRAW NEW EDGE

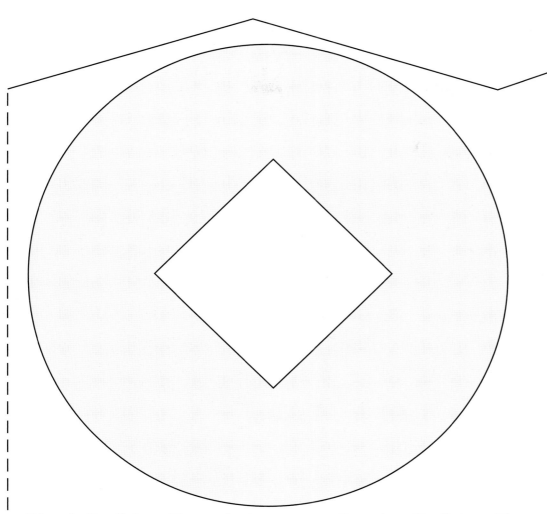

Block Quilting Template:

• Cut a 6″ square of freezer paper and pre-shrink.

• Trace **circle with square hole** template to paper side and cut on lines.

• Press, shiny side down on quilt with a dry iron centering over nine-patch block.

• Stitch beside paper's inside edge and outside edge then peel up and reuse on each block.

Border Quilting Template:

• Cut a 16″x 20″ piece of freezer paper and pre-shrink.

• Fold in half in both directions.

• Place folds on dashed template lines and trace zig-zag lines.

• Fold freezer paper into quarters so that drawn lines can be seen.

• Staple every three inches just outside zig-zag line.

• Cut on lines.

• Center template over quilt using fold lines as guides, press in place with a dry iron, and stitch next to zig-zag edge.

Baby Feathers
Susan K Cleveland
14½"x 14½", 2005

Baby Feathers

This little feathered star is so precious. It requires careful cutting, sewing, and pressing, so please don't begin thinking this is a quick project. It will take patience but will be worth the effort.

Solid hand-dyed fabrics showcase precision piecing and thread work, and a dark background allows the lighter feathers to jump off the quilt and sparkle.

Four fabrics are used as features. A gradation of color or value will give a wonderful effect. When *Feature 1* is lightest in value and *Feature 4* is darker, it seems the star is glowing. I cut all features from one piece of graded hand-dyed fabric. With careful cutting, I was able to get four features from one piece!

Fabric etc.	Needed	Sample	Yours	Cut
background	½yd	hand-dyed Peacock from Cherrywood Fabrics		see next page
features	(4) scraps	feature 1: yellow (center) feature 2: yellow-orange feature 3: orange-pink feature 4: pink (kite & outer diamond)		see next page
backing & batting	fat quarter			18"x 18"
binding	fat quarter	Peacock		as desired

decorative thread for quilting
piping fabric: fat quarter; 1⁄16" cording: 3yds (optional)
freezer paper

Fabric requirements are based on fabrics 40"–44" in width.
A fat quarter measures approximately 18"x 20" and a fat eighth approximately 9"x 22".
Starch all fabrics before cutting.
All seam allowances are ¼".
Piped binding instructions are written in great detail in Piping Hot Binding. See "Resources" on page 110.

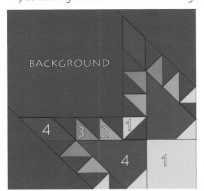

Use this as a guide for fabric choices and placement.

Cut Background Fabric

Cut strips on lengthwise grain, parallel to selvage. Strips will be approximately 18″ in length.

- Cut (1) 4⅛″ strip, then cut into (4) 4⅛″ squares, label *corners*.

- Cut (4) 1¾″ strips, label *borders*.

- Cut (2) 1¾″ strips, then cut into (20) squares, label *background feathers*.

- Cut (2) 3″ strips, cut those strips into:

    » (17) 3″x ⅞″ pieces, label *pieced border*

    » (3) 3″x 2″ pieces, label *pieced border*

    » (3) 3″x 1¾″ pieces, label *pieced border*

- Cut (1) 7″ strip, and from that strip, cut:

    » (1) 7″ square, cut diagonally twice, label *sides*

    » (8) 1½″ squares, cut diagonally once, label *feather background*

Cut Feature Fabrics

Feature 1:

- Cut (1) 3⅛″ square, label *center*.

- Cut (2) 1⅝″ squares cut diagonally once, label *center triangles*.

- Cut (4) 1¾″ squares, label *feathers*.

- Cut (6) 3″x ⅞″ pieces, label *pieced border*.

Feature 2:

- Cut (8) 1¾″ squares, label *feathers,*.

- Cut (5) 3″x ⅞″ pieces, label *pieced border*.

Feature 3:

- Cut (8) 1¾″ squares, label *feathers*.

- Cut (6) 3″x ⅞″ pieces, label *pieced border*.

Feature 4:

- Pre-shrink an approximate 5″x 10″ piece of freezer paper. Using template, carefully cut (8) kite shapes from freezer paper. This is finished size. Seam allowances are added when fabric is cut.

- Press (8) freezer paper kite templates to **wrong side** of fabric and cut fabric ¼″ from edge of template. Leave freezer paper on fabric.

- Cut 1⅛″ strip then cut 45 degree diamonds from strip. (Make 45 degree cut on one end, then measure 1⅛″ from fresh cut to make diamonds. See diagram.)

- Cut (6) ⅞″x 3″ pieces, label *pieced border*.

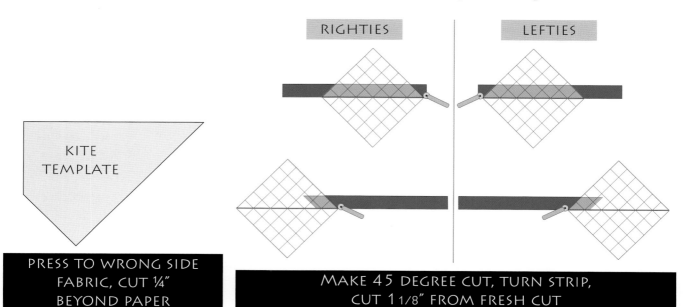

RIGHTIES   LEFTIES

KITE
TEMPLATE

PRESS TO WRONG SIDE
FABRIC, CUT ¼″
BEYOND PAPER

MAKE 45 DEGREE CUT, TURN STRIP,
CUT 1 1/8″ FROM FRESH CUT

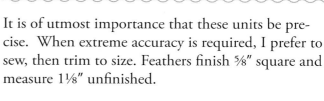

FEATURE 1 — MAKE 4
FEATURE 2 — MAKE 8
FEATURE 3 — MAKE 8

MAKE 8
MAKE 16
MAKE 16

Make Feathers

It is of utmost importance that these units be precise. When extreme accuracy is required, I prefer to sew, then trim to size. Feathers finish ⅝″ square and measure 1⅛″ unfinished.

• Pair each *Feature 1*, *Feature 2*, and *Feature 3* feather square (1¾″) with a same-sized background square, right sides together. Draw a line diagonally then sew with tiny, 1.5mm stitches ¼″ each side of the drawn line. Cut on the line and press seam allowances **open**.

• Trim each triangle square to exactly 1⅛″ taking care that the seam extends through the square's corners.

Assemble Feather Units

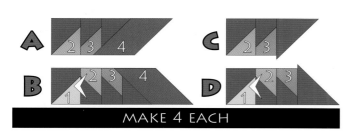

MAKE 4 EACH

• Carefully make (4) of each feather unit using all feathers and diamonds. Press seam allowances **open** to distribute bulk unless otherwise noted with an arrow. Points of triangles must be ¼″ from edge.

Assemble Corner Units

• Add unit A, then unit B to *corner* background squares, press in direction of arrows. (The *corner* square was cut large so the star's points float in the background.) Trim corners of square in line with diamond's edge. Repeat to make 4 units.

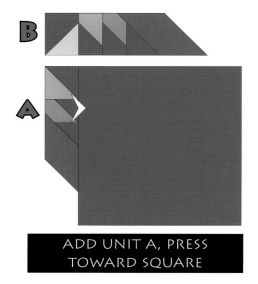

ADD UNIT A, PRESS TOWARD SQUARE

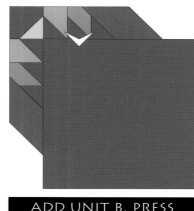

ADD UNIT B, PRESS TOWARD SQUARE

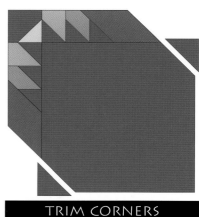

TRIM CORNERS OF SQUARE

Assemble Side Units

• Using partial seams, add *unit C*, then *unit D* to *sides* background pieces, press in direction of arrows. Sew only the portion of seam marked with a bold line when adding units C & D.

• Add kite using freezer paper as guide to be sure kite's tip matches corner of unit C.

• Add *Feature 1 center triangles* to another kite. Press to kite.

• Add *kite/triangle unit* to *side unit*. Press to *kite/triangle unit*.

• Repeat to make 4 units.

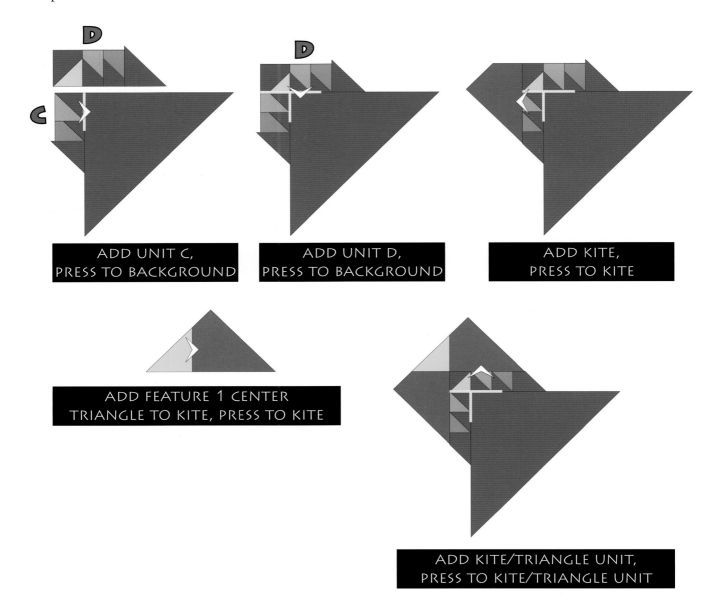

ADD UNIT C,
PRESS TO BACKGROUND

ADD UNIT D,
PRESS TO BACKGROUND

ADD KITE,
PRESS TO KITE

ADD FEATURE 1 CENTER
TRIANGLE TO KITE, PRESS TO KITE

ADD KITE/TRIANGLE UNIT,
PRESS TO KITE/TRIANGLE UNIT

Assemble Top/Bottom Rows

• Move background triangle out of the way, add *corner units* to *side units* then complete partial seams. Press toward big background triangle. Repeat to make 2.

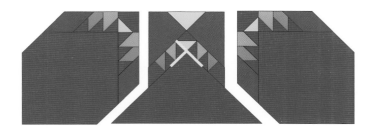

**ARRANGE
2 CORNER UNITS & 1 SIDE UNIT**

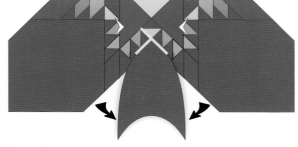

**SEW, PRESS TO SIDE UNIT (KITE)
THEN COMPLETE PARTIAL SEAMS,
PRESS TOWARD BACKGROUND TRIANGLE**

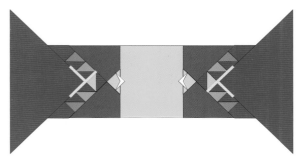

**ADD SIDE UNITS TO CENTER SQUARE,
PRESS TO CENTER SQUARE**

Assemble Middle Row

• Add *side units* to *center square*. Press toward *center square*.

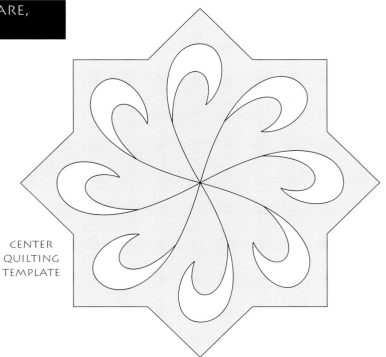

CENTER
QUILTING
TEMPLATE

Join Rows

- Move background triangles out of the way, add top row and complete partial seams. Repeat for bottom row.

Tip: Use the Wacker tool to flatten bulky seam allowances (and release pent up emotions). A flat quilt is much easier to quilt and looks so nice.

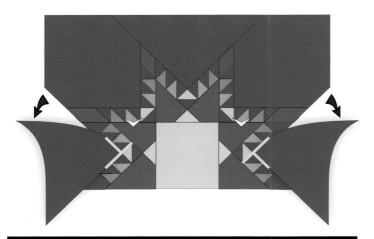

ADD TOP ROW TO MIDDLE ROW, PRESS TOWARD MIDDLE ROW

COMPLETE PARTIAL SEAMS, PRESS TOWARD BACKGROUND, REPEAT FOR BOTTOM ROW

Build Pieced Border Strip Sets

Each pieced border strip set will be used twice. See *"Skinny Pieced Borders"* on page 24 for details or read ahead if the suspense is eating you up.

- Collect 3″ background pieces of various widths labeled *pieced border*, and (23) feature pieces labeled *pieced border*.

- Arrange as you like, alternating backgrounds and features. Choose 2 feature pieces for corners. They will be added later.

- With 1.5mm stitches sew border strip sets as shown pressing seam allowances open. Notice one border strip uses 2″x 3″ background pieces and the other uses 1¾″x 3″ background pieces. Note: Corner pieces are not added until later.

- Label each strip set, and record the length of each strip set.

Tip: Each pieced border strip set will be added to the quilt, then trimmed to correct width. This eliminates the pieced border's tendency to stretch.

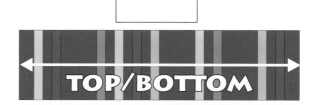

BUILD TOP PIECED BORDER STRIP SET, USE 2″-WIDE & 7/8″-WIDE BACKGROUNDS

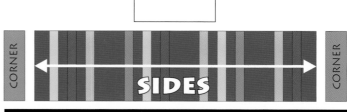

BUILD SIDE PIECED BORDER STRIP SET, USE 1¾″-WIDE & 7/8″-WIDE BACKGROUNDS

STEAM, SQUARE QUILT BODY, RECORD MEASUREMENTS

ADD CORNERS TO SIDE PIECED BORDER STRIP SET

Add Pieced Borders to Quilt

Tip: Since piecing is rarely perfect, it's best to piece borders, then adjust either the border or body of quilt to fit perfectly.

• Steam block and whack the daylights out of the bulky intersections if you have a Wacker. See *"Resources"* on page 110. Square up block to create straight, clean edges.

• Mark top of quilt with a pin (or a mark in the seam allowance) so length and width can be distinguished.

• Measure quilt body width and length through the center and record. At this point in time, the measurements should be the same. If quilt is wider than *top/bottom* border strip set, trim width of quilt to match *top/bottom* border. If quilt is smaller, open a seam in the border strip set beside one of the wide background strips and trim wide strip as necessary.

• Repeat for quilt length and *side* border strip set.

• Add corner pieces to *sides* strip set and press toward corner pieces. (Corner pieces were cut earlier as ⅞"x 3" feature fabrics and labeled *pieced border*.)

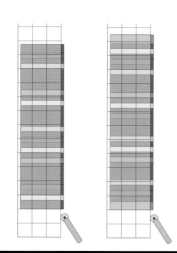

• Trim one long edge of each border strip set to create straight, clean edges to be sewn to the quilt body. Take care that seams are parallel to lines on ruler.

TRIM ONE LONG EDGE OF EACH PIECED BORDER STRIP SET

- Sew trimmed edge of *top/bottom* border strip set to top of quilt body, press toward quilt body, then trim border ⅝" from seam line. It may be necessary to remove the pin noting "top of quilt", but that's OK at this point. Repeat with leftover strip set to bottom of quilt body (sew, press, trim).

- Sew trimmed edge of *sides* border strip set to side of quilt body/border being careful to match seams at corner pieces, press toward quilt body, then trim border ⅝" from seam line. Repeat with leftover strip set for second side.

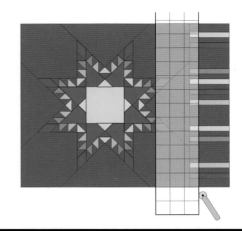

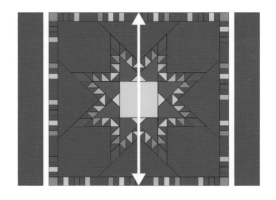

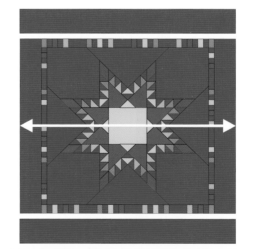

Add Outer Border

- Measure length of quilt then cut two *border* pieces this length. These strips were cut earlier but were not cut to length.

- Sew *border* pieces to sides of quilt pressing seam allowances toward outer border.

- Measure new width of quilt and cut two *border* pieces this length. These strips were cut earlier but were not cut to length.

- Sew *border* pieces to top and bottom of quilt pressing seam allowances toward outer border.

Quilt

- Layer quilt top, batting and backing. Press so layers cling together. Pin layers together and stitch with long stitch length through all layers near each edge of quilt top. This stitching will protect edges from stretching during quilting.

- I suggest using a thin silk or cotton thread to quilt in the ditch of border seams that are not pressed open.

- For decorative quilting I used YLI #30 silk thread.

Finish

- Draw quilt's new edge 1¼" from outer border seam. Binding or piping will be placed along this new edge.

- For binding instructions, please see *"Binding"* on page 38 or refer to *Piping Hot Binding*, a booklet containing very detailed instructions for finishing quilts with a beautiful piped binding.

- Label your quilt.

SEW PIECED BORDER SIDE STRIP SET TO TOP OF QUILT, PRESS, TRIM EXCESS

APPLY OUTER BORDER (MEASURE, CUT TO SIZE, SEW, PRESS, REPEAT)

Quilting Templates:

- Cut three 5" squares of freezer paper and pre-shrink.

- Trace **square with swirl, triangle with swirl, and center quilting** templates to paper side of freezer paper and cut on lines. Center quilting template is on page 55. Each template will be a shape with cut-outs—like a stencil.

- Press, shiny side down on quilt with a dry iron.

- Stitch beside paper's edge then peel up and reuse.

- Note: When stitching where the paper is just a slit, peel up one side and stitch **beside** paper. Don't stitch in a slit.

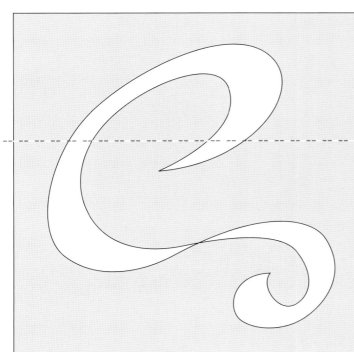

Border Quilting Templates:

- Cut two 16" squares of freezer paper and pre-shrink.

- Fold each piece in half in both directions.

- Place folds on dashed template lines and trace zig-zag lines (red on one piece, blue on the other).

- Fold freezer paper into quarters so that drawn lines can be seen.

- Staple every three inches just outside lines.

- Cut on line.

- Center template over quilt using fold lines as guides, press in place with a dry iron, and stitch next to edge.

Japanese Daisies
Susan K Cleveland
11"x 20", 2011

Japanese Daisies

This project has the illusion of a border but the center is actually a sheer fabric stitched over a solid background piece. I love appliqueing daisies with a heavy decorative thread, and I chose a matching color for a more subtle effect. This gives texture at the edges of the appliquéed pieces but not a bold outline.

Quilting is a major element here given the amount of background fabric. I chose Spagetti 12wt cotton in the Baby Lock Sashiko machine for a hand quilted look and I love it. Each stitch is two threads and the space between stitches really is a space! Quilting the sheer area baffled me so I stitched beads to give it a tufted look.

Of course, the edge needed a little dressing up, and decorated, embellished prairie points scattered willy nilly tucked under piping in the binding seemed just right. Ahhh. This little piece is one of my absolute favorites. Please see its sister quilts on pages 106 and 107.

Fabric etc.	Needed	Sample	Yours	Cut
background	fat quarter	navy		12"x 21"
sheer	fat eighth	light blue organza		6"x 13"
daisies	fat quarter	red		use templates
daisy centers	scraps	acid green		use templates
prairie points	fat eighth	acid green		2½"x at least 16"
backing & batting	fat quarter			14"x 23"
binding	fat quarter	navy		as desired

Pellon Decor-Bond or fusible web
decorative thread for applique and quilting
felted wool balls and beads, beading thread (optional)
piping fabric: fat quarter; ¹⁄₁₆" cording: 2yds (optional)
freezer paper

Fabric requirements are based on fabrics 40"–44" in width.
A fat quarter measures approximately 18"x 20" and a fat eighth approximately 9"x 22".
Starch all fabrics before cutting.
All seam allowances are ¼".
Piped binding instructions are written in great detail in Piping Hot Binding. Please see Resources on page 110.

Applique

- Pull strands of sheer fabric from edges to fray about ⅜" of each edge.

- Place sheer onto background 3¼" from bottom edge and 2¼" from side as shown and carefully pin in place.

- Prepare daisies and centers per templates on pages 63 *and* 64.

- Place largest daisy as shown moving pins as necessary.

- If fusible web is used, fuse in place according to manufacturer's instructions. If Decor-Bond is used, simply press in place so layers cling a bit. (Adjust iron temperature if necessary to avoid damaging sheer.)

- Applique as you like. I used a blanket stitch (2mm wide and 3mm in length) by machine with WonderFil Spagetti 12wt cotton thread and stitched each flower petal, then jumped to the next petal. Please see *Decorative Thread Applique on page 18 and Machine Stitching on page 34.*

- Add other flowers and centers, removing pins as necessary.

Tip: Before adding flower center, iron a small piece of wool batting and steam flat. Cut a piece slightly smaller than flower center and place wool just under flower center. This makes the flower center poof a bit.

FRAY SHEER,
PLACE ON BACKGROUND, PIN,
PLACE AND APPLIQUE DAISIES

Quilt

- Layer quilt top, batting and backing. Press so layers cling together. Pin layers together and stitch with long stitch length through all layers near near each edge of quilt top. This stitching will protect edges from stretching during quilting.

- Cut piece of freezer paper 5" x 12", center over sheer and press in place.

- Quilt through all layers beside paper beginning and ending at flowers' edges. Pull threads to wrong side, tie off and bury tails in layers of quilt. Remove freezer paper.

- With thin thread, quilt around flower petals and centers. I stitched around petals and when I hit the center, I stitched along it and then out around next petal …

LAYER QUILT TOP/BATTING/BACKING,
PIN THEN STITCH EDGES,
CUT, PLACE FREEZER PAPER, THEN

**DRAW NEW EDGE,
PLACE PRAIRIE POINTS**

• Make background quilting template per page 65 and quilt on background only. A heavy decorative thread will give great impact. Pull quilting threads to wrong side, tie off and bury tails in layers of quilt. Remove remaining freezer paper. I used the Baby Lock Sashiko machine for a hand quilted look.

⟩ *Tip: This template could also be used to mark quilting lines.*

• In the sheer section, stitch X's or beads between flowers.

Finish

• Make prairie points with 2½″ strips that were cut earlier. Please see *Prairie Points: plain/embellished on page 36* for details. Embellish if you like.

• Draw quilt's new edge creating about an 11″ x 20″ rectangle. Binding or piping will be placed along this new edge.

• Baste or glue prairie points along quilt's new edge aligning cut edges with drawn lines.

• For binding, please see *Binding on page 38* or refer to *Piping Hot Binding*, a booklet containing very detailed instructions for finishing quilts with a beautiful piped binding. I used a ½″-wide finished piped binding with binding strips cut 3¾″.

• Label your quilt.

2

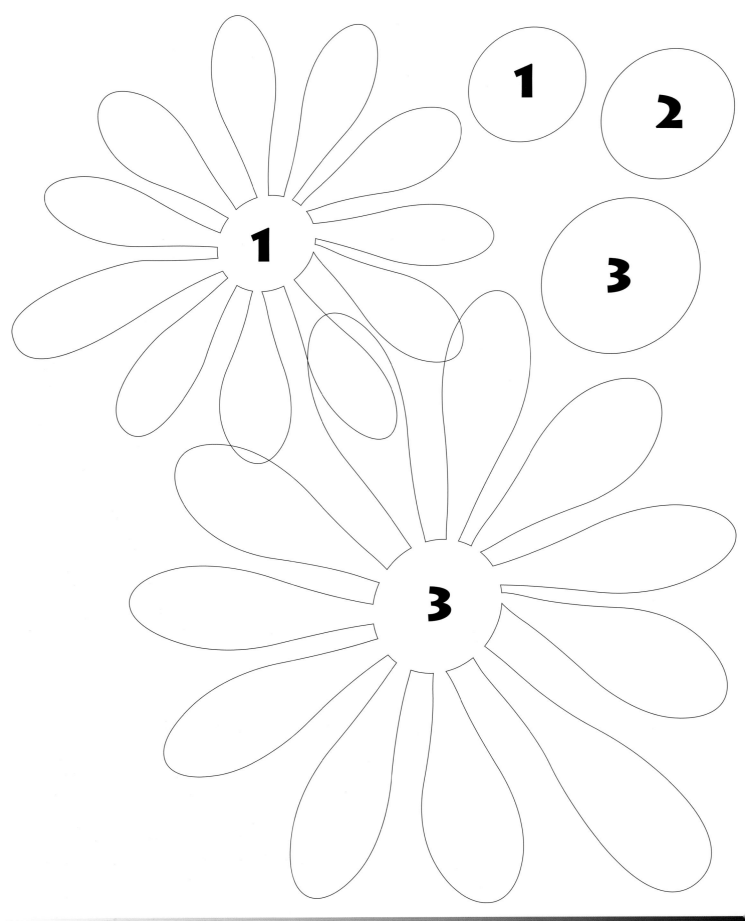

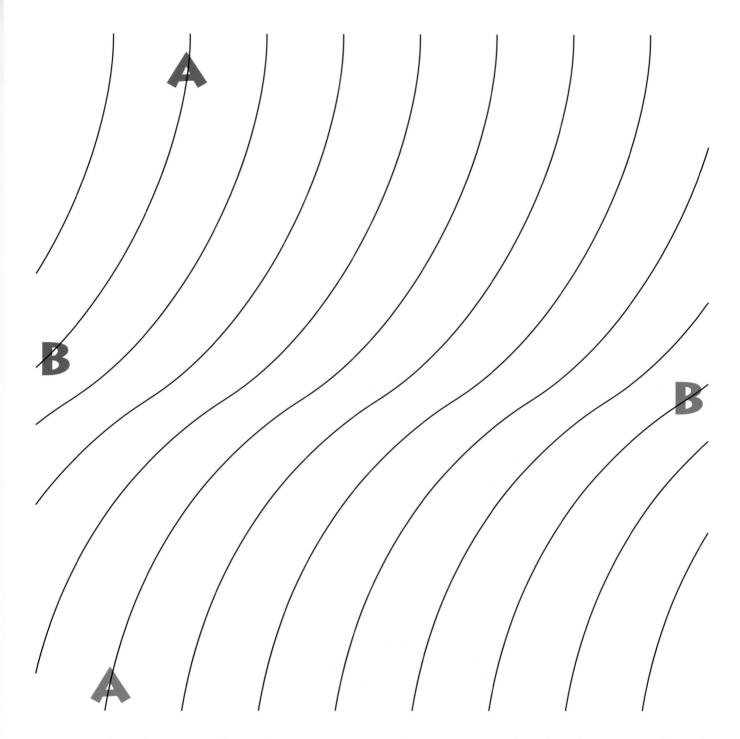

To use background quilting template:

• Cut piece of freezer paper 21″ x 12″ and draw lines ½″ in from edge of paper.

• Fill square with wavy lines. Trace wavy lines, then move red "A" to match blue "A" to repeat pattern and do the same with "B" until box is filled.

• Cut paper on wavy lines but do not cut within ½″ of paper's edge.

• Place freezer paper quilting template over quilt and press with dry iron to adhere freezer paper to quilt.

• Tear away one wavy strip and quilt beside paper's edge. Repeat for entire quilt. Begin/end quilting lines at daisy's edges and sheer fabric's edges. (Do not quilt through daisies or sheer fabric.)

Happy Daisy
Susan K Cleveland
9"x 11", 2009

Happy Daisy

When a quick, but super cute piece is needed, this is the "go to" project. It can be dressed up or dressed down, embellished or just simple and precious.

Of course, the edge needs a little dressing up, and just a few decorated, embellished prairie points tucked under piping in the binding do the trick. My friends tell me they had great fun with this project. Please see pages 106 and 107.

Fabric etc.	Needed	Sample	Yours	Cut
background	fat quarter	black/white print		11"x 13"
daisy	8" square	red		use template
large heart	scrap	acid green		use template
small heart	scrap	purple		use template
prairie points	scraps	acid green & purple		(5) 2" squares
backing & batting	fat quarter			12"x 14"
binding	fat quarter	black/white print		as desired

Pellon Decor-Bond or fusible web
decorative thread for applique and quilting
piping fabric: fat quarter; ¹⁄₁₆" cording: 1½yd (optional)
freezer paper

Fabric requirements are based on fabrics 40"–44" in width.
A fat quarter measures approximately 18"x 20" and a fat eighth approximately 9"x 22".
Starch all fabrics before cutting.
All seam allowances are ¼".
Piped binding instructions are written in great detail in Piping Hot Binding. Please see Resources on page 110.

Applique

- Prepare daisy and centers per templates on page 69.

- If fusible web is used, fuse in place according to manufacturer's instructions. If Decor-Bond is used, simply press in place so layers cling a bit. Please see *Decorative Thread Applique on page 18*.

- Applique daisy then each center heart as you like. I used a blanket stitch (2mm wide and 3mm in length) by machine with Wonder-Fil Spagetti 12wt cotton thread and stitched each flower petal, then jumped to the next petal. Please see *Machine Stitching on page 34*.

} *Tip: Before adding flower centers, iron a small piece of wool batting and steam flat. Cut pieces slightly smaller than flower centers and place wool just under each flower center before appliqueing. This makes flower centers poof a bit.*

APPLIQUE FLOWER ON
BACKGROUND,
THEN ADD CENTERS

Quilt

- Layer quilt top, batting and backing. Press so layers cling together. Pin layers together and stitch with long stitch length through all layers near each edge of quilt top. This stitching will protect edges from stretching during quilting.

- Quilt around flower petals and centers. Heavy thread will add a glow around the flower while thin thread will be more subtle.

- Make freezer paper template of quilt's final shape per template on page 69 and press to right side of quilt. Mark new edge by drawing or stitching a line beside freezer paper. Remove freezer paper but do not cut quilt. The exposed bias edges could stretch.

- Quilt background. I simply hand quilted parallel wavy lines.

STITCHING TO
STABILIZE QUILT

LAYER QUILT,
PIN THEN STITCH EDGES,
QUILT AROUND MOTIFS

Finish

- Make prairie points from pieces cut earlier. Please see *Prairie Points: plain/embellished on page 36* then baste or glue prairie points along quilt's drawn edge.

- For binding, please see *Binding on page 38* or refer to *Piping Hot Binding*, a booklet containing very detailed instructions for finishing quilts with a beautiful piped binding.

- After a trim or binding has been sewn beside the drawn edge, then extra quilt top/batting/backing may be cut away.

- Label your quilt.

NEW EDGE OF QUILT

MARK WAVY EDGE,
PLACE PRAIRIE POINTS

To use quilt shape template:

• Cut approximate 12″ square of freezer paper and fold in half.

• Unfold then lay fold over dashed line. Trace template, rotate to trace other half, then cut on solid lines.

African Octet
Susan K Cleveland
10½"x 16½", 2011

Octet

Think prairie points are only used as precious accents here and there? This piece *features* lined prairie points and they very much deserve the spotlight, don't you think? They're very easy to create but you don't need to tell your friends.

Because the background fabric is a print, quilting is less noticed except for the inner border where a simple line with a heavy thread does the job nicely. Stitching on the prairie points is optional. The stitching that shows on this example is done with the Baby Lock Sashiko machine and WonderFil Spagetti 12wt cotton. A hand quilting stitch with double thread and large stitches will give similar results.

Embellishing prairie points with beads is great fun. Please heed the voice of experience. If you wish your beads to dangle, then stitching beads to prairie points before piecing PPs into the quilt is easier than adding them later. I like to hide knots inside the prairie points.

Fabric etc.	Needed	Sample	Yours	Cut
background/ outer border	fat quarter	stripe		(7) 5½"x 1¾" pieces, label *background #2–8* (1) 5½"x 2¾" piece, label *background #1* (1) 5½"x 1½" piece, label *background last* (4) 2"x at least 17" pieces, label *outer border*
prairie point main	scraps	Madagascar from Cherrywood Fabrics		(8) 1¾"x 3½" pieces all same or different
prairie point lining	scrap	brown		(8) 2¼"x 3½" pieces
inner border	scrap	brown		(2) 1½"x at least 13" pieces (2) 1"x at least 8" pieces
foundation (hidden in project)	scrap	muslin		at least 6"x 13"
backing & batting	fat quarter			13"x 19"
binding	fat quarter	stripe		as desired

decorative thread for embellishing prairie points and quilting
beads, beading thread (optional)
piping fabric: fat quarter; ¹⁄₁₆" cording: 2yds (optional)
permanent fabric glue (optional)
fabric or permanent markers
Prairie Pointer pressing tool (highly recommended)

Fabric requirements are based on fabrics 40"–44" in width.
A fat quarter measures approximately 18"x 20" and a fat eighth approximately 9"x 22".
Starch all fabrics before cutting.
All seam allowances are ¼".
Piped binding instructions are written in great detail in Piping Hot Binding. Please see "Resources" on page 110.

Make prairie points

• Stitch each prairie point main fabric to a prairie point lining piece right sides together along a 3½″ edge to create 3½″ squares. Press seam allowance toward main fabric. Make (8).

• Fold and press each pieced square in half parallel to seam, wrong sides together.

PIECE PPS,
PRESS TOWARD MAIN

• Stitch through both layers near fold with heavy decorative threads if desired. Please see *"Machine Stitching"* on page 34.

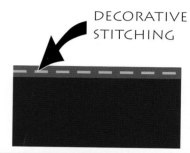

DECORATIVE STITCHING

FOLD AND PRESS IN HALF,
ADD DECORATIVE STITCHING
(OPTIONAL)

• Fold into prairie points as described in *"Prairie Points"* on page 36.

• Add beads if you like.

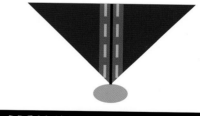

PRESS INTO PRAIRIE POINTS,
ADD BEAD (OPTIONAL)

Tip: There are two options for adding beads at prairie point tips.

One is for dangling beads. Adding beads in this manner is more easily done before they are sewn into the project as I suggest hiding knots inside prairie points (PPs).

Another option is to stitch beads during quilting which involves stitching through all layers of the quilt and the PP tips. They don't dangle with this option.

In either case, pass needle and thread down and up through beads twice.

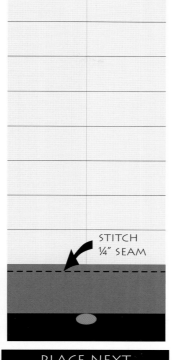

MARK FOUNDATION, PLACE FIRST BACKGROUND & PP

STITCH ¼" SEAM

PLACE NEXT BACKGROUND, SEW

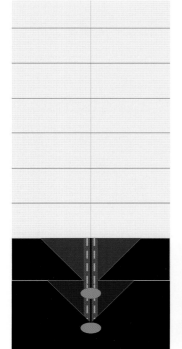

FLIP BACKGROUND UP, PLACE NEXT PP

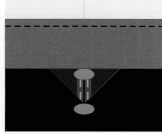

PLACE NEXT BACKGROUND, SEW

Piece quilt body

• Starch foundation fabric until very stiff, then cut 5½" x 12½" piece.

• With a thin permanent marker, draw a line 2¾" from bottom edge. If your background fabric (not foundation) is very light in color and shadowing is a concern, make these marks lightly so they don't show through.

• Add 7 more lines at 1¼" intervals. Top section will be only 1" wide.

• Add line down center.

• Place widest background piece (labeled #1) right side up along bottom edge of foundation and pin in place.

• Center bottom prairie point along top edge of background fabric and glue or baste in place.

Tip: If your machine skips stitches sewing through so many layers, try using a walking foot.

Tip: Move the machine's needle so it's ¼" from the right edge of the foot, then stitch aligning right edge of foot with fabric's edge.

• Place 1¾" background (one labeled #2–8) over PP right side down and pin in place.

• Stitch through all layers ¼" from edge of fabric.

• Press strip upward. It should reach next line or be very close. If is doesn't, adjust seam allowance for remaining seams.

• Continue adding PPs and background strips until foundation is covered. Always align with drawn line if background fabric doesn't quite reach line. Last strip used will be the 1½" (labeled "last").

Add Inner Border

Tip: When measuring a quilt body, use the same ruler that will be used to trim borders to length.

Tip: Measure a quilt through the center rather than along one edge. The edge may have stretched. The center measurement will yield more accurate results.

• Measure length of quilt and cut (2) 1½"-wide inner border pieces this length. These strips were cut earlier but were not cut to length.

• Sew inner border pieces to sides of quilt pressing seam allowances toward border.

• Measure new width of quilt and cut (2) 1"-wide inner border pieces this length. These strips were cut earlier but were not cut to length.

• Sew inner border pieces to top and bottom of quilt pressing seam allowances toward new border.

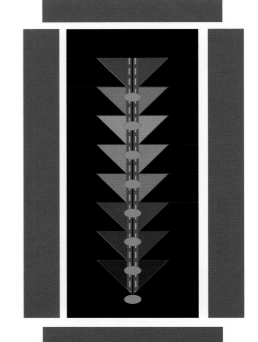

INNER BORDER

Add Outer Border

• Measure length of quilt and cut (2) 2"-wide outer border pieces this length. These strips were cut earlier but were not cut to length.

• Sew outer border pieces to sides of quilt pressing seam allowances toward border.

• Measure new width of quilt and cut (2) 2"-wide outer border pieces this length. These strips were cut earlier but were not cut to length.

• Sew outer border pieces to top and bottom of quilt pressing seam allowances toward new border.

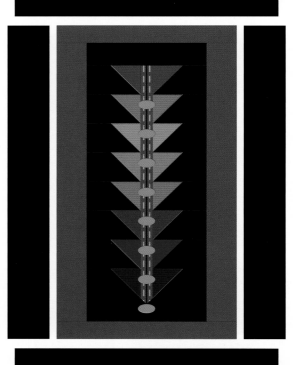

OUTER BORDER

LAYER, STAY-STITCH, QUILT

Quilt

• Layer quilt top, batting and backing. Press so layers cling together. Pin layers together and stitch with long stitch length through all layers near each edge of quilt top. This stitching will protect edges from stretching during quilting.

• I suggest using a thin silk or cotton thread to stitch in the ditch of border seams and in horizontal seams where prairie points are inserted. Simply lift prairie points out of the way.

• For decorative quilting I used the decorative thread used to embellish prairie points and stitched a crazy, giant zig-zag in the outer border and a simple straight stitch in the inner border.

Finish

• Draw quilt's new edge 1½" from border outer seams. Binding or piping will be placed along this new edge.

• For binding, please see *"Binding"* on page 38 or refer to *Piping Hot Binding*, a booklet containing very detailed instructions for finishing quilts with a beautiful piped binding.

• Label your quilt.

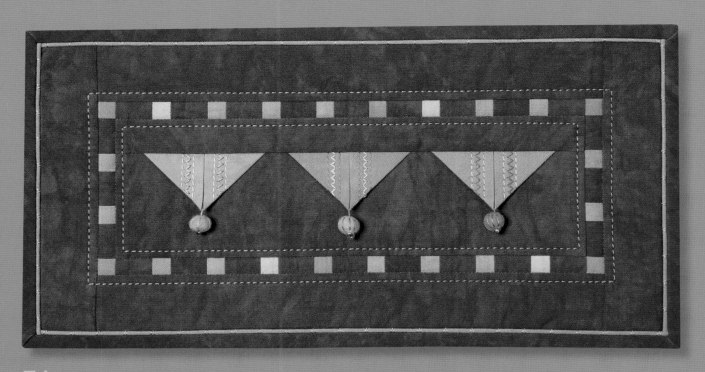

Trio
Susan K Cleveland
13½"x 6¾", 2008

Trio

Again, I believe prairie points can be the main attraction. These are stitched and beaded for extra ooo-la-la and are surrounded by a tiny ⅜" pieced border. (It's not as hard as you think.)

Quilting is subtle but does get noticed. Finishing takes on more importance in a small quilt. Oh, and why not embellish the embellishments? These felted wool balls are embellished with heavy silk thread.

Fabric etc.	Needed	Sample	Yours	Cut
background	fat quarter	turquoise		*cut strips parallel to selvage* (1) 3½"x 11" piece, label *lower body* (1) 1¼"x 11" piece, label *upper body* (3) 2"x at least 16" pieces, label *outer border* (12) 1¼"x 3" pieces, label *pieced border*
features	scraps	pink/orange/green/aqua		(12) ⅞"x 3" pieces, label *pieced border* (many of each color) (3) 3" squares, label *prairie points*
backing & batting	fat quarter			16"x 9"
binding	fat quarter	turquoise		as desired

decorative thread for embellishing prairie points and quilting
beads, beading thread (optional)
piping fabric: fat quarter; 1/16" cording: 2yds (optional)
permanent fabric glue (optional)
Prairie Pointer pressing tool (highly recommended)

Fabric requirements are based on fabrics 40"–44" in width.
A fat quarter measures approximately 18"x 20" and a fat eighth approximately 9"x 22".
Starch all fabrics before cutting.
All seam allowances are ¼".
Piped binding instructions are written in great detail in Piping Hot Binding. Please see "Resources" on page 110.

Make Prairie Points

- Fold and press each prairie point square in half, wrong sides together.

- Stitch through both layers near fold with heavy decorative threads if desired. Please see *"Machine Stitching"* on page 34.

- Fold into prairie points as described in *"Prairie Points"* on page 36.

- Beads may be added later. Adding them now makes trimming the quilt difficult.

MAKE 3 PRAIRIE POINTS

Assemble Quilt Body

- Pin or glue prairie points (PPs) to right side of lower body along long edge. Centers should be 3″ apart.

- Sew upper body piece along edge with PPs.

} Tip: If your machine skips stitches sewing through so many layers, try using a walking foot.

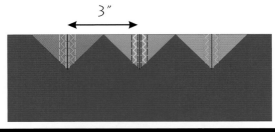

PLACE PPS

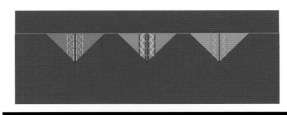

SEW LOWER BODY
TO UPPER BODY

Piece Borders & Sew to Quilt Body

Each pieced border strip set will be used twice. See *"Skinny Pieced Borders"* on page 24 for details or read ahead if the suspense is eating you up.

- Arrange *pieced border* pieces as shown or in another arrangement you like. The short strip set will be used for side borders and the long will be used for top/bottom borders. Two feature pieces left over will become corner pieces.

- Piece together with 1.5mm stitches and press seam allowances open to distribute bulk.

} Tip: Stitching with a short stitch length for seams to be pressed open will greatly lessen the chance that threads will show in the seam line.

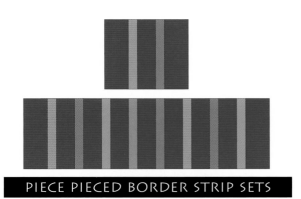

PIECE PIECED BORDER STRIP SETS

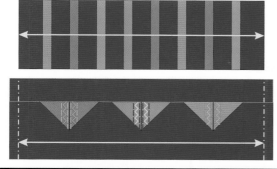

**MEASURE LONG STRIP SET,
TRIM QUILT BODY WIDTH TO MATCH**

• Measure length of long border strip set and trim quilt body width to match. Make sure to keep center PP centered.

} *Tip: Since piecing is rarely perfect, it's best to piece borders, then adjust either the border or body of quilt to fit perfectly.*

**MEASURE SHORT STRIP SET, TRIM
QUILT BODY HEIGHT TO MATCH**

• Measure length of short border strip set and trim quilt body length to match. Trim from lower body only.

**ADD CORNER PIECES TO
SHORT BORDER STRIP SET**

• Add corner pieces to short border strip set. Stitch with 2.0mm stitches and press seam allowances toward corner pieces so seam allowances nest when border is sewn to quilt body.

Add Pieced Border

• Trim one edge of each pieced border to make a clean, straight edge on each strip set. Check to be sure seams are parallel to lines on the ruler. (This clean, straight edge will be sewn to the quilt body.)

{ *Tip: There's a trick to sewing skinny borders. Please see "Skinny Pieced Borders" on page 24.*

• Sew clean, straight edge of long pieced border to top edge of quilt body and press seam allowance toward quilt body.

• Trim pieced border ⅝″ from border seam. Border will finish ⅜″.

• With remaining long pieced border, repeat for bottom of quilt. (Sew, press, trim ⅝″ from border seam.)

• Repeat for side borders taking care to match seam intersections at corners. (Sew, press, trim ⅝″ from border seam.)

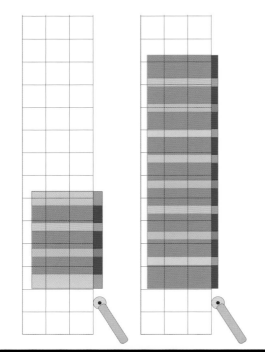

TRIM PIECED BORDERS

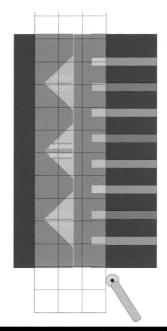

SEW LONG PIECED BORDER TO TOP OF QUILT, THEN TRIM (REPEAT FOR BOTTOM)

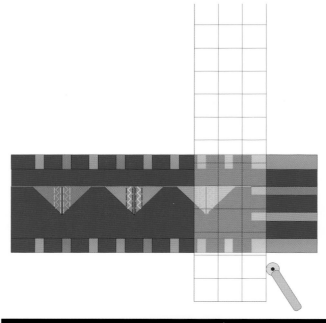

SEW SHORT PIECED BORDER TO SIDE OF QUILT, THEN TRIM (REPEAT FOR OTHER SIDE)

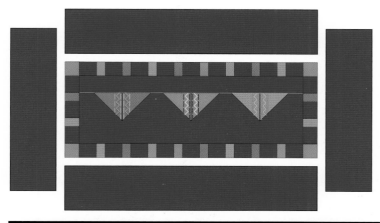

OUTER BORDER:
MEASURE, CUT TO LENGTH, SEW TO QUILT,
TOP/BOTTOM FIRST, THEN SIDES

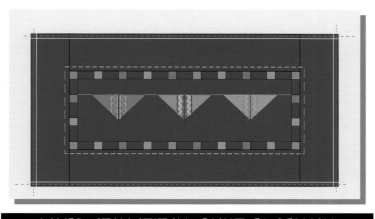

LAYER, STAY-STITCH, QUILT, EMBELLISH

Finish

• Draw quilt's new edge 1½" from outer border seam. Binding or piping will be placed along this new edge.

• For binding, please see *"Binding"* on page 38 or refer to *Piping Hot Binding*, a booklet containing very detailed instructions for finishing quilts with a beautiful piped binding.

• Label your quilt.

Add Outer Border

• Measure width of quilt then cut two outer border pieces this length. These strips were cut earlier but were not cut to length.

• Sew outer border pieces to top and bottom of quilt pressing seam allowances toward outer border.

• Measure new length of quilt and cut two outer border pieces this length. These strips were cut earlier but were not cut to length.

• Sew outer border pieces to sides of quilt pressing seam allowances toward outer border.

Quilt & Embellish

• Layer quilt top, batting and backing. Press so layers cling together. Pin layers together and stitch with long stitch length through all layers near each edge of quilt top. This stitching will protect edges from stretching during quilting.

• I suggest using a thin silk or cotton thread to quilt in the ditch of border seams.

• For decorative quilting I used the same decorative thread used to embellish prairie points and stitched ⅛" inside and outside of the pieced border.

• Sew beads to prairie point tips.

Tip: There are two options for adding beads at prairie point tips.

One is for dangling beads. Hide knots inside prairie points (PPs).

Another option is to stitch beads through all layers of the quilt and the PP tips. They don't dangle with this option.

In either case, pass needle and thread down and up through the beads twice.

Prairie Point Pillow
Susan K Cleveland
14"x 14", 2010

Prairie Point Pillow

This project can take on so many personalities, and they're all fantastic! Three sizes are included from the adorable 7″, the ever-popular 14″, and the bold 20″. Fabrics you choose determine the personality of your pillow and the opportunities for embellishing are tremendous. I can't resist Cherrywood Fabrics 8-step gradation, Carnival. It makes me happy.

Of course, if you'd rather, this pillow top may be transformed into a quilt or incorporated into a tote.

Fabric	Needed	Sample	Yours	Cut
back-ground	small: fat eighth **medium: fat quarter** **large: ¾yd**	black/white print		small: (2) 2½″ x 9″, (7) 1⅛″x 9″ **medium: (1) 5¼″x 16″, (1) 4¼″x 16″, (7) 1½″x 16″** **large:(1) 8″x 24″, (1) 6″x 24″, (7) 2″x 24″**
prairie points	small: total fat quarter **medium: ½yd** **large: total ¾yd**	8-step gradation		(starch until *very* firm) small: (8) 2″x at least 13″ or (44) 2″squares **medium: (8) 3″x at least 18″ or (44) 3″ squares** **large: (8) 4½″x at least 27″ or (44) 4½″ squares**
foundation (light-colored fabric)	small: 10″ square **medium: 17″ square** **large: 25″ square**	muslin		(starch until *very* firm) small: 9″ square **medium: 16″ square** **large: 24″ square**
backing	small: 9″ square **medium: 16″ square** **large: 24″ square**			If you already know how to insert a zipper and wish to do so, cut backing wider to account for seam allowances. Zipper instructions are not included.

decorative thread for embellishing prairie points
beads, beading thread (optional)
ric-rac or piping cording: small 1yd; medium 2yds; large 3yds your preferred size
piping fabric: fat quarter (optional)
permanent fabric glue (highly recommended)
fusible interfacing: same size as backing
freezer paper: same size as backing
pillow form or stuffing or crushed walnut shells (small only)
fabric or permanent markers in two colors that will show on foundation
Prairie Pointer pressing tool (highly recommended)

Fabric requirements are based on fabrics 40″–44″ in width.
A fat quarter measures approximately 18″x 20″ and a fat eighth approximately 9″x 22″.
Starch all fabrics before cutting.
All seam allowances are ¼″.

Make Prairie Points

MAKE 44 PRAIRIE POINTS

- Fold and press each prairie point strip (or square) in half wrong sides together lengthwise.

- Stitch through both layers near fold with heavy decorative threads if desired. Please see *"Machine Stitching"* on page 34.

- Cut into segments same size as strip cut width. (small 2″, medium 3″, large 4½″)

- Fold into prairie points as described in *"Prairie Points"* on page 36.

- Beads may be added now or later.

Prepare Foundation

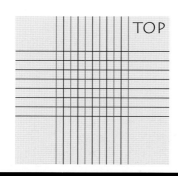

PREPARE FOUNDATION

If your background fabric is light-colored, and shadowing might be a problem, mark lightly on the foundation so lines don't show through.

- Label top of pillow.

- Draw horizontal lines (total 8 lines):

    small: bottom line 2½″ from bottom edge, then (7) more lines ⅝″ apart

    medium: bottom line 5¼″ from bottom edge, then (7) more lines 1″ apart

    large: bottom line 8″ from bottom edge, then (7) more lines 1½″ apart

- Draw black vertical lines (total 5 lines):

    all sizes: draw black vertical line down center

    small: add (2) lines on each side ¾″ apart

    medium: add (2) lines on each side 1½″ apart

    large: add (2) lines on each side 2¼″ apart

- Draw red vertical lines (total 6 lines):

    all sizes: draw red vertical lines between black lines

    small: add red lines ⅜″ right and left of outermost black lines

    medium: add red lines ¾″ right and left of outermost black lines

    large: add red lines 1⅛″ right and left of outermost black lines

Build Pillow Top - sew & flip

I used different color prairie points for each row but feel free to mix it up as you like.

• Place widest background strip on foundation below bottom horizontal line (right side up).

• Place prairie points (PPs) along edge of strip centering on **black** vertical lines with prairie point folds facing upward (or down if you prefer). Glue or baste in place.

• Place narrow background strip over PPs (right side down), sew with ¼" seam allowance.

Tip: Adjust the needle position on your machine so the needle is ¼" from the right edge of the foot then sew with the cut edges of fabrics at edge of foot.

Tip: If your machine skips stitches sewing through so many layers, try using a walking foot.

• Flip narrow strip up and press. The cut edge should be aligned with or within ⅛" of next horizontal line. If it is not, adjust machine's needle position for a smaller seam allowance.

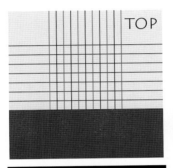

PLACE BACK-GROUND STRIP

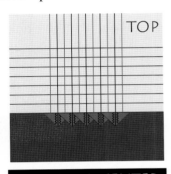

PLACE PPS, CENTER ON BLACK LINES

PLACE NEXT BACK-GROUND, SEW

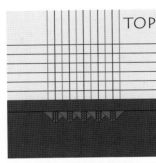

FLIP BACKGROUND UP, PRESS

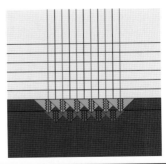

PLACE NEXT ROW OF PPS CENTERING ON RED LINES

• Place prairie points (PPs) along next horizontal line centering on **red** vertical lines with prairie point folds facing upward (or down if you prefer). Glue or baste in place.

• Continue until foundation is covered. Alternate using **black/red** vertical lines. For large and medium pillows last background strip will be wider than strips 2–7.

Apply Trim

• Make pillow shape template with freezer paper.

• With a dry iron press freezer paper (shiny side down) to right side of pillow top centering prairie points under freezer paper.

• For piped edge, make piping using the thickness of cording you prefer. See *"Perfect Piping"* on page 20.

• Begin at pillow's bottom edge. Place points of ric-rac or fold of piping at freezer paper's edge. Stitch through center of ric-rac or exactly over piping stitching line.

• When returning to beginning, bend beginning tail into seam allowance, overlap ½", then bend ending tail into seam allowance.

MAKE PILLOW TEMPLATE, PRESS TO RIGHT SIDE PILLOW, APPLY RIC-RAC

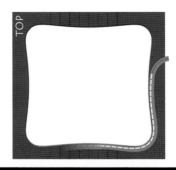

MAKE PILLOW TEMPLATE, PRESS TO RIGHT SIDE PILLOW, APPLY PIPING

Finish Pillow

• Remove freezer paper.

• Apply fusible interfacing to wrong side pillow backing fabric. (If you know how to insert a zipper, do so now using larger backing piece cut earlier.)

• Place pillow top (with ric-rac or piping) over backing with right sides together. Pin.

• Using ric-rac or piping stitching line as a guide, sew through all layers one thread left of stitching but leave an opening for turning and stuffing (larger opening is needed for pillow form, smaller opening for walnut shells).

• Trim seam allowances to ⅜".

• Turn right-side out.

• Insert pillow form or stuffing. Crushed walnut shells may be used for small pillow. Extra stuffing may be needed in corners.

• Hand stitch opening closed.

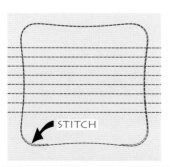

STITCH

RIGHT SIDES TOGETHER, SEW JUST INSIDE RIC-RAC OR PIPING STITCHING LINE (LEAVE OPENING FOR TURNING)

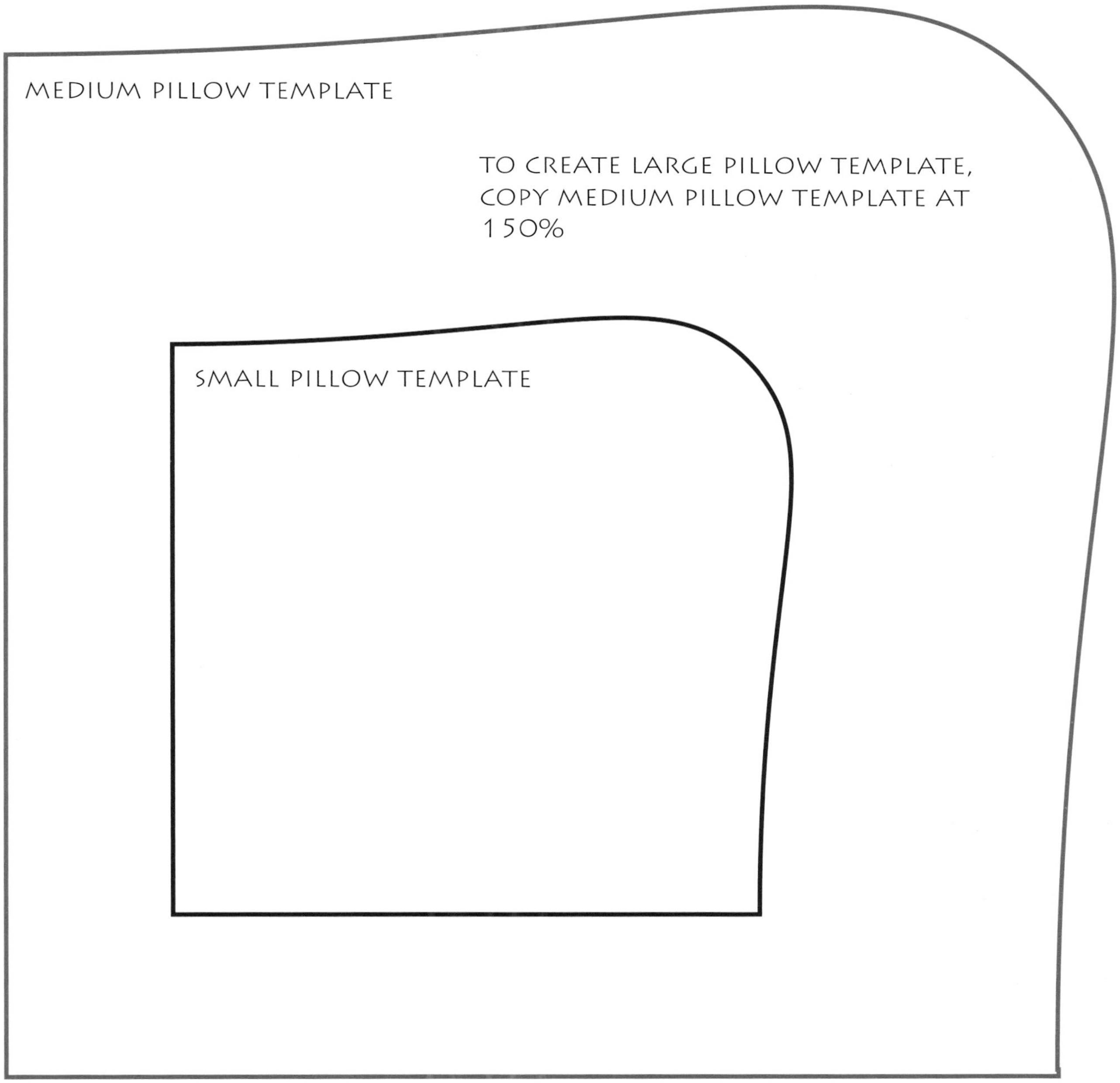

MEDIUM PILLOW TEMPLATE

TO CREATE LARGE PILLOW TEMPLATE,
COPY MEDIUM PILLOW TEMPLATE AT
150%

SMALL PILLOW TEMPLATE

Pillow Template:

- Cut a piece of freezer paper approximately same size as pillow top and pre-shrink.

- Fold in half in both directions.

- Place folds on dashed template lines and trace curved lines

- Fold freezer paper into quarters so that drawn lines can be seen.

- Staple every three inches just outside drawn line.

- Cut on line and un-fold.

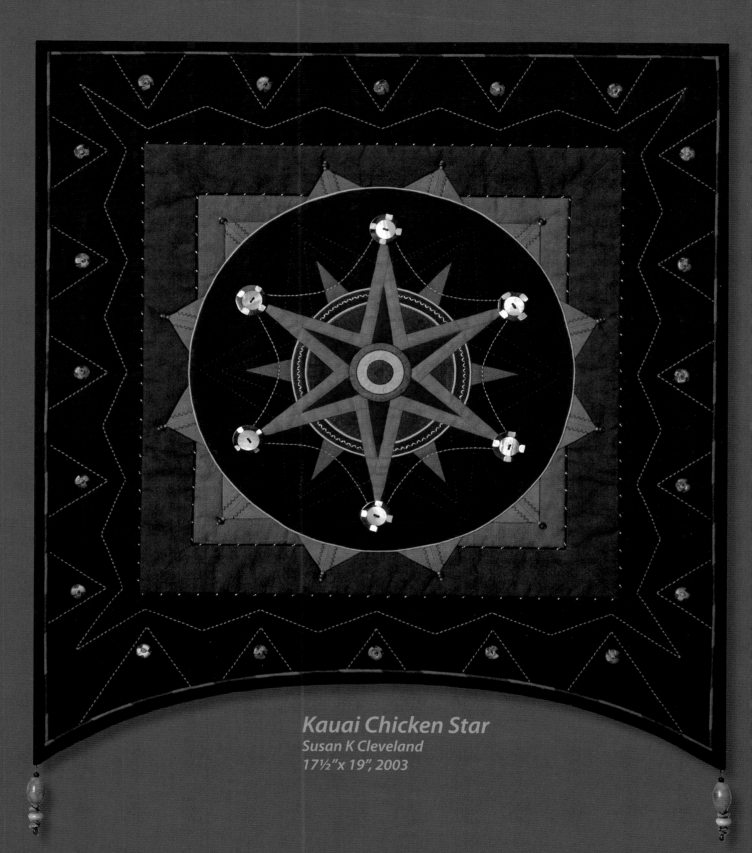

Kauai Chicken Star
Susan K Cleveland
17½"x 19", 2003

Kauai Chicken Star

This is my favorite quilt. It incorporates all my favorite tricks in one detailed piece. Each element is so very important on a quilt of this small scale that eliminating one special tidbit would lessen the whole package. I chose to feature hand-dyed solid fabrics in order to show off threads and embellishments to their fullest.

Take your time with this piece and enjoy every scrumptious moment.

Fabric etc.	Needed	Sample	Yours	Cut
background/ outer border	½yd	black		see next page for background cutting (3) 3¼" x 20", (1) 6"x 20" label **outer border**
star points star outline background star	scraps	purple orange olive		see next page
small background circle	4½" square	teal		approximate 4½" square, heavily starched
large background circle	5" square	purple		approximate 5" square, heavily starched
circle piping	fat quarter	gold		1¼" bias strips adding up to 2yds
prairie points	fat eighth	orange		2½" strips adding up to at least 30"
background square	fat quarter	olive		starch heavily then cut exact 10" square
inner border	fat quarter	teal		(4) 2"x 13"
piping in borders	fat quarter	embellished black		1¼" bias strips adding up to 120"
backing & batting	fat quarter			21"x 22"
binding	fat quarter	black		as desired

decorative thread for quilting and embellishing prairie points, thin thread for ditch stitching
beads and buttons
piping fabric for binding: fat quarter; ⅟₁₆" cording: 3yds (optional)
cording <⅟₁₆" for border seam piping and circle piping: 3yds
freezer paper
circle cutter or compass

Fabric requirements are based on fabrics 40"–44" in width.
A fat quarter measures approximately 18"x 20" and a fat eighth approximately 9"x 22".
Starch all fabrics before cutting.
All seam allowances are ¼" unless otherwise noted.
Piped binding instructions are written in great detail in Piping Hot Binding. See "Resources" on page 110.

Piece Star

Freezer paper piecing lesson: Pre-shrink freezer paper by ironing it to pressing surface (shiny side down), cool, remove from pressing surface. Trace template shapes then cut freezer paper templates. Templates do not include seam allowances. Press to wrong side fabric then cut fabric precisely ¼" outside templates except on curved edges where a ½" seam allowance is better. Place pieces right sides together using pins to check alignment and sew with 2.0mm stitches beside freezer paper extending seams to fabric's edges. Turquoise arrows indicate alignment and turquoise dashed lines represent the seam to be sewn.

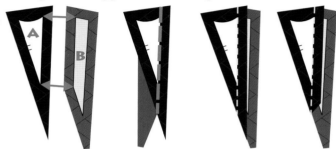

- Prepare star pieces A, B, C, D, E as described above. Do not remove freezer paper.

- Piece AB and CDE units sewing beside paper but from edge of fabric to edge of fabric, press seam allowances as shown. Trim points (dog ears) that extend. Make 6 each. Do not remove freezer paper.

PIECE AB UNITS (MAKE 6)

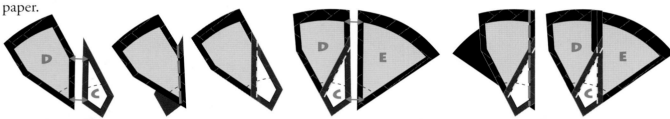

PIECE CDE UNITS (MAKE 6) ... LAST SEAM: CLIP TO PRESS BACKGROUND OPEN

- Make 35" of piping for circles behind star (gold in sample) and trim seam allowance to ¼". See *"Making Piping"* on page 20. To save time, make another 35" of piping for circle outside of star.

- Press a 3½" circle of triple-thick freezer paper to right side small background circle fabric (teal in sample) and create piped circle per *"Piping Hot Curves"* on page 22. Repeat for 4¼" circle of freezer paper on large background circle fabric (purple in sample). Do not remove freezer paper. Piping ends may simply butt up rather than overlap.

- Remove freezer paper from large piped circle, carefully center small piped circle over large piped circle aligning piping beginning/endings, tape in place, stitch in ditch of small circle (removing tape as necessary). Do not remove freezer paper.

- Add decorative stitching between pipings, then remove paper. See *"Stitching Heavy Threads"* on page 34 for details.

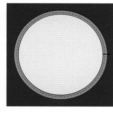

SEAMS PRESSED TO BACK

PIPE SMALL BACKGROUND CIRCLE, REPEAT FOR LARGE BACKGROUND CIRCLE

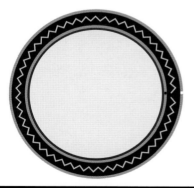

STACK PIPED CIRCLES, STITCH DITCH OF SMALL CIRCLE, ADD DECORATIVE STITCHING

- Trace piped wedge template to paper side of 4¼″ circle of freezer paper (single layer), press to right side stacked piped circles making sure piping beginning/endings aren't under a wedge, cut wedges (freezer paper/ fabric/piping). Do not remove paper. On piped wedges, trim away large circle from underneath small.

- Tape piped wedges on right side CDE, stitch in ditch of large piped circle, remove paper wedges. Make 6.

PREPARE PIPED WEDGES THEN ADD PIPED WEDGES TO CDE UNITS (MAKE 6)

- Add F to CDE. Press toward F. Make 6.

- **Begin to assemble star with partial seam**. Align registration marks, press seam allowances toward F.

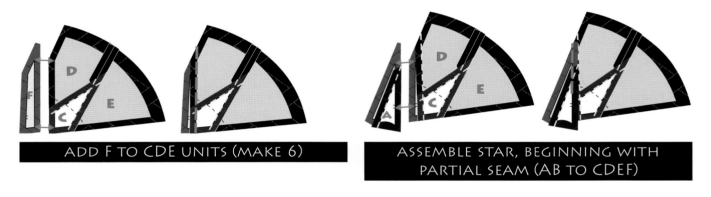

ADD F TO CDE UNITS (MAKE 6)

ASSEMBLE STAR, BEGINNING WITH PARTIAL SEAM (AB TO CDEF)

- Continue piecing counter-clockwise from wrong side, align registration marks. Stitch edge to edge. Add CDEF, then AB … After last piece is added, join to make circle then complete partial seam. This gets awkward. Hang in there!

- Remove freezer paper (warm with iron, sweep ball-point awl or stiletto under paper to loosen, use tweezers to grab paper bits).

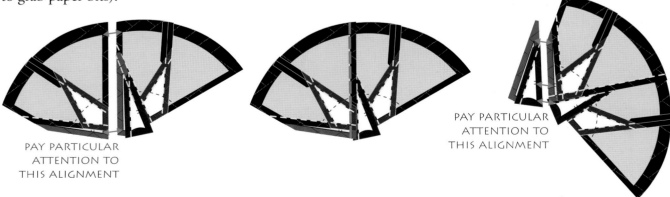

PAY PARTICULAR ATTENTION TO THIS ALIGNMENT

PAY PARTICULAR ATTENTION TO THIS ALIGNMENT

ADD CDEF, THEN ADD AB, THEN ADD CDEF, …

Applique Center Circles

• Cut double-thick freezer paper circles ⅝″, 1⅛″, 1½″ and use a paper punch to punch a hole near the center of each.

• Follow *"Circle Applique-invisible"* technique on page 16 to applique small circle (teal in sample) to 4″ square of middle circle (gold in sample) then remove circle template.

• Applique assembly (small/medium) onto 4″ square of large circle fabric (green in sample), remove template … Note: When pulling up running stitch, take care to center small circle over medium template.

• Stitch around small and medium circles with a heavy thread for accent. This will be done on the largest circle during quilting through all layers.

• Applique assembly (small/medium/large) to star unit. Note: When gathering running stitch, take care to center small/medium circles over large template.

APPLIQUE CENTER CIRCLE ASSEMBLY

Build Background/Borders

Normally when borders are mitered, multiple borders are sewn together then added to the quilt. When piping is inserted in border seams, this cannot be done because mitering piping would not be a pleasant experience. The following is a very odd mitering technique and one that I use only when piping is inserted into a mitered border.

• I used embellished piping in these border seams. See *"Tip: Embellished piping"* on page 20 if you're interested. Make at least 48″ very tiny piping (with less than 1/16″ cording) for border seams following *"Perfect Piping"* instructions on page 20. Trim seam allowance to ¼″. Another 60″ will be needed when second border is added. Save some set-up time and make that piping now also.

• Sew piping to each side of center square (10″ square, green in sample). Cross over in corners and stitch exactly over piping stitching line. Trim excess piping extending beyond corners of square.

• One at a time, pin ***inner border*** piece to quilt body (right sides together) matching center of side to center of border. To sew, flip over and sew one thread left of piping stitching line beginning and ending at intersections of piping stitching lines. Back stitch or use very tiny 1.0mm stitches at beginning and ending of each seam. Press seam allowance toward border. Repeat for each side being careful not to catch previous border in new seam.

• Press all border seams and trim excess border lengths at corners as shown.

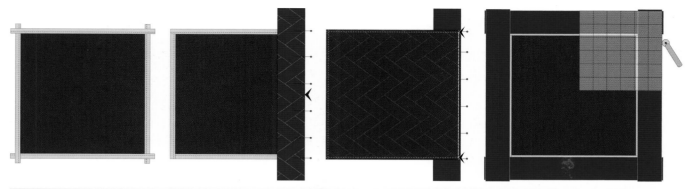

APPLY PIPING, PIN BORDER, SEW BORDER, TRIM EXCESS AT CORNERS

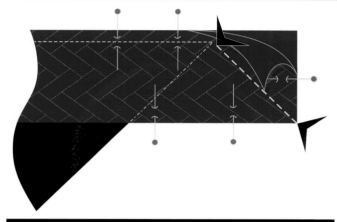

MITER FIRST BORDER CORNERS

• Miter corners by placing neighboring borders right sides together and tucking quilt body down between the borders. Draw a line from end of border seam to corner of border as shown. Begin stitching on line ⅛" from border seam and continue to corner with tiny, 1.5mm stitches. (The ⅛" gap allows room for piping.) Press seam allowances open and trim to about ⅜". Note: Another way to fold before sewing is to fold the quilt body wrong sides together diagonally and let the borders flop right sides together.

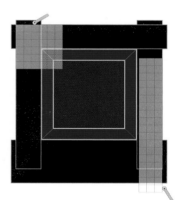

TRIM EXCESS OUTER BORDER LENGTH

• Repeat applying piping and applying border for *outer border*. Bottom border piece will be wider than others.

• Trim excess border lengths at top corners same as *inner border*. Trim excess of bottom border as shown.

• Miter top two corners the same as *inner border*.

• Since one border is wider, the bottom corner miters will be different. When mitering bottom two corners, pin with narrow border on top. Draw a line from end of border seam to **intersection of side border and end of bottom border** as shown. Begin stitching on line ⅛" from border seam with tiny, 1.5mm stitches. (The ⅛" gap allows room for piping.) Press seam allowances open and trim to about ⅜". Bottom left corner will be reverse of diagram and will need to be sewn in opposite direction.

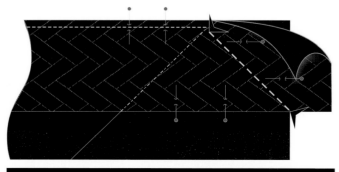

MITER BOTTOM CORNERS

Add Star to Background

• Make (12) prairie points from strips cut earlier per *"Prairie Points - plain/embellished"* on page 36. Beads may be added later.

• Make 33″ piping (gold in sample) unless this was sewn earlier.

• Trace **Star & Prairie Point Placement template** onto paper side of pre-shrunk freezer paper, then make triple-thick freezer paper template. See page 20.

• Make marks near edges of star unit showing where star points point.

• Press template to right side of star using marks for proper placement.

• Pipe star circle per *"Piping Hot Curves"* on page 22. Note: Where piping comes back to beginning, bend beginning tail into seam allowance, continue stitching to overlap about ¼″–½″, then bend ending tail into seam allowance and take a couple more stitches.

• Center piped star circle over background/borders carefully checking alignment. Tape in place.

• Tuck prairie points under piped circle and glue in place. Allow ⅞″ of each prairie point's center fold to extend beyond piping.

• Stitch in ditch between piping and star background to secure star and prairie points removing tape as necessary. Stitch with a tiny, 2.0mm stitch length, a very thin thread and a 60/8 Microtex needle for best results.

• Trim background from behind star circle. Remove freezer paper template. Feel very, very proud of yourself.

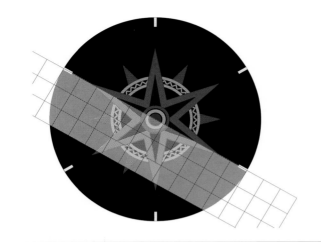

MARK STAR POINTS

PIPE STAR CIRCLE

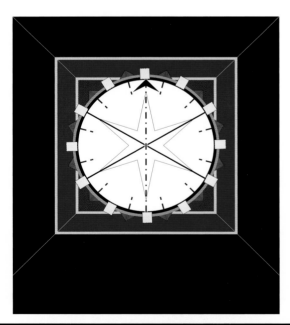

PLACE STAR, TUCK PRAIRIE POINTS UNDER, STITCH DITCH

Quilt Shape Template

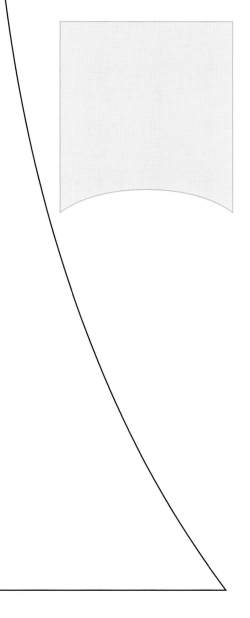

- Add this template (doubled) to 18½" square freezer paper.

- Press to quilted quilt.

- Mark beside template to draw quilt's new edge where piping or binding will be placed.

Quilt

- Machine quilt in ditches with thin thread (star pieces, curved piping ditches, borders). See *"In-the-ditch Quilting"* on page 26 for details.

- Quilt with heavy decorative thread around large center circle. See *"Stitching Heavy Threads"* on page 34 and *"Decorative Quilting - machine"* on page 28 for details.

- Make freezer paper templates for quilting designs (stars in background, and swoops). There are 3 different templates to be traced.

- One at a time, press each template to quilt, stitch beside template with heavy decorative thread on background fabric only, remove template. Yes, there are many starts and stops, but it's worth it. Please see *"Stitching Heavy Threads"* on page 34 and *"Beginning and Ending"* on page 28 for more information.

- For twisted thread illusion, whip swoops with second color heavy thread in a tapestry needle. Please see "Twisted Thread Illusion" on page 35 for details.

- Quilt border as you wish.

Finish

- Make freezer paper template for quilt's shape, press to finished quilt. Mark new edge.

- Bind quilt with plain binding ala *"Plain Binding"* on page 38, or see *Piping Hot Binding* in *"Resources"* on page 110 for detailed instructions on piped bindings.

- Add embellishments at star tips, in border, and at prairie point tips.

- Add tassels at bottom corners.

- Add label.

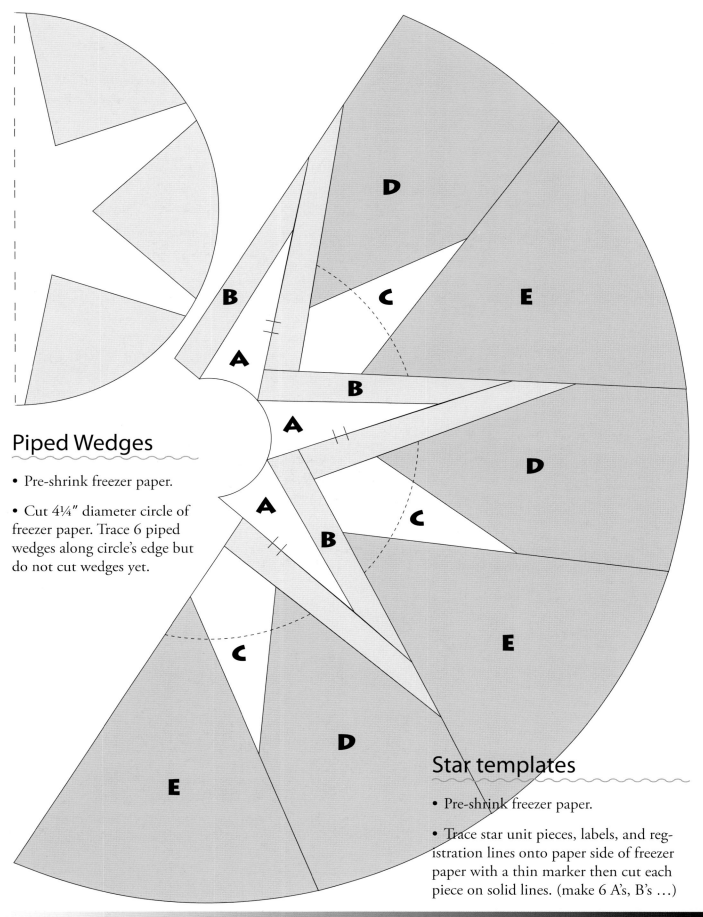

Piped Wedges

- Pre-shrink freezer paper.

- Cut 4¼″ diameter circle of freezer paper. Trace 6 piped wedges along circle's edge but do not cut wedges yet.

Star templates

- Pre-shrink freezer paper.

- Trace star unit pieces, labels, and registration lines onto paper side of freezer paper with a thin marker then cut each piece on solid lines. (make 6 A's, B's …)

Star and Prairie Point Placement

- Pre-shrink (3) approximate 11″ squares of freezer paper.

- Trace template twice on one sheet to make full circle.

- Press one plain pre-shrunk piece of freezer paper to pressing surface. Press another plain piece over it, then press the traced piece over both.

- Peel off of pressing surface

- Cut on curved line to make triple-thick freezer paper template.

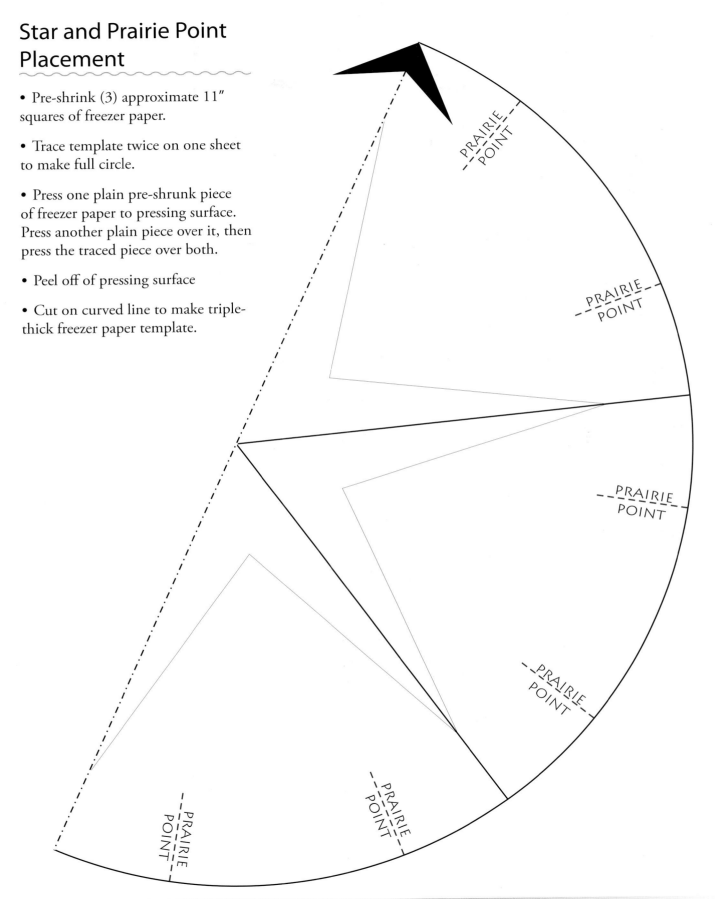

Quilting templates

• Pre-shrink (3) at least 11″ squares freezer paper.

• Trace one shape (doubled at dotted line) to each piece.

• Cut on solid lines.

Gallery

Psychedelic Big Bang
Susan K Cleveland, 75"x 47", 2010
original design

Bouncin'
Susan K Cleveland, 63"x 61, 2005
original design

Carnival Star
Susan K Cleveland, 64"x 82", 2003
original design

Spangled Star Banner
Susan K Cleveland, 58"x 80"x 2002
original design

Twirling Tassels
Susan K Cleveland, 54"x 61", 2001
original design

Party of Three
Susan K Cleveland, 56"x 45", 2000
original design

Pretty Flaky
Susan K Cleveland, 41"x 41", 1999
original design

Beth Holec

Kim Klocke

Sharon Sandberg

Synneva Hicks

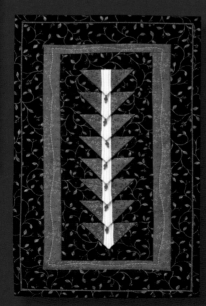

Judy Plank

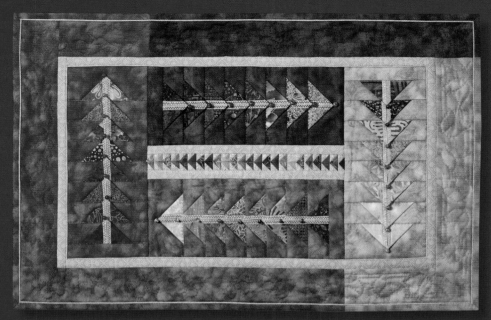

Maureen Ruskell

Enid Gjelten Weichselbaum

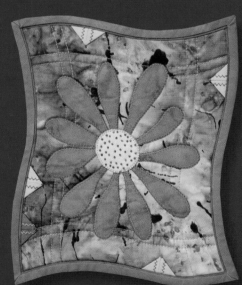

Leitha Bothun

Norma Sherwood

Hippie Daisies, Susan K Cleveland

Heather Holtan

Lynne Majka

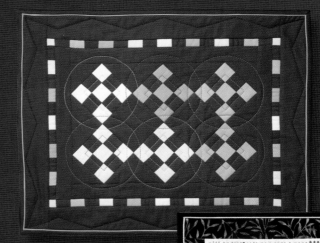

Julie Antolak

Susan K Cleveland

Beth Holec

**©2011 Enid Gjelten
Weichselbaum**

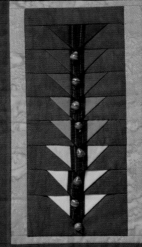

**Enid Gjelten
Weichselbaum**

Kim Klocke

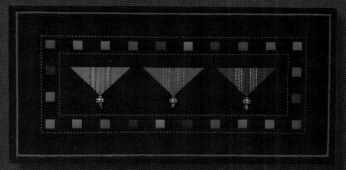

Susan K Cleveland

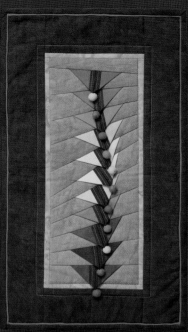

Enid Gjelten Weichselbaum

Barb Lovett

Judy Plank

Barb Lovett

Lynne Majka

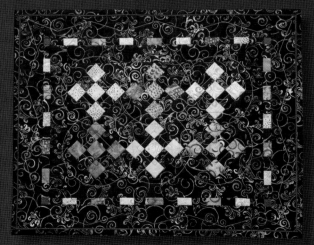

Norma Sherwood

Resources

I encourage you to visit your favorite quilt shop for supplies and please let your local shop owner know about wonderful supplies/books/tools you learn about through your quilting experiences.

Tools

• Pieces Be With You®, www.PiecesBeWithYou.com (*Piping Hot Binding*, Groovin' Piping Trimming Tool, and most of the tools listed in *"Supplies"* on page 6)

• Karen Kay Buckley, www.karenkaybuckley.com (Perfect Circles, Perfect Scissors, Instructional DVDs, …)

• www.steadybetty.com (Steady Betty pressing surface)

• www.harvesthousefabrics.com (Wacker seams perfect tool)

• www.spiraleyeneedles.com (a new, better self-threading needle)

Hand-dyed fabrics

• Cherrywood Fabrics Inc., www.CherrywoodFabrics.com or 888-298-0967

• Laura Wasilowski, www.artfabrik.com (threads and hand-dyed fabrics)

• Ricky Tims, www.RickyTims.com

• Frieda Anderson, www.friestyle.com

Threads

• Pieces Be With You®, www.PiecesBeWithYou.com (WonderFil Spagetti 12wt cotton)

• WonderFil threads, www.wonderfil.net

• Superior Threads, www.superiorthreads.com or 800-499-1777

• YLI Corp., www.ylicorp.com

• Laura Wasilowski, www.artfabrik.com (threads and hand-dyed fabrics)

• Nancy Eha, www.beadcreative.com (beading thread and beads)

Embellishments

• Handbehg Felts, www.Handbehg.com (felted wool balls and other adornments)

• River Silks, www.riversilks.com, click "Retailers" (silk ribbon)

Books

• *Piping Hot Binding (booklet, tool, cording)* by Susan K Cleveland, published by Pieces Be With You

• *Piping Hot Curves* by Susan K Cleveland, published by Pieces Be With You

• *Marvelous Miters* by Susan K Cleveland, published by Pieces Be With You

• *Hand Applique with Embroidery* by Sandra Leichner, published by American Quilter's Society, www.sandraleichner.com

• *Fanciful Stitches* by Laura Wasilowski, published by C&T Publishing, www.artfabrik.com

• *Garden Whimsy Applique* by Mickey Depre, published by American Quilter's Society, www.mdquilts.com

• *Threadplay* by Libby Lehman, published by Brewer Publications

• *Machine Quilting with Decorative Threads* by Maurine Noble and Elizabeth Hendricks, published by Martingale & Company

• *Foolproof Machine Quilting* by Mary Mashuta, published by C&T Publishing

• *Threadwork Unraveled* by Sarah Ann Smith, published by American Quilter's Society

Index

Author

Susan's enthusiasm for quilting is said to be contagious and she's thrilled to share her quilts and techniques with others. There's always serious fun included in her workshops and programs as well as an abundance of valuable information.

Her distinctive original designs have been receiving awards at national and international shows since 1999. She's taught at major quilt conferences, appeared on television and internet shows, authored magazine articles, authored *Piping Hot Binding*, invented the Groovin' Piping Trimming Tool and Prairie Pointer tool, and authored and published *Piping Hot Curves* and *Marvelous Miters*. Currently, the Quilter's Custom Seam Guide is in development.

Visit **www.PiecesBeWithYou.com** to see more quilts and see what's new with Susan.

Princess of Piping and Prairie Points

Tiara designed and created by dear friend, Queen Elizabeth Holec